Purdue University Press Series in the History of Philosophy

General Editors

Adriaan Peperzak
Robert Bernasconi
Joseph J. Kockelmans
Calvin O. Schrag

~WITNESSING HEAVEN~

True Stories of Transformation from
Near-Death Experiences

Transformed
by Heaven

EDITORS OF GUIDEPOSTS

Transformed by Heaven

Published by Guideposts Books & Inspirational Media
100 Reserve Road, Suite E200
Danbury, CT 06810
Guideposts.org

ACKNOWLEDGMENTS

Every attempt has been made to credit the sources of copyrighted material used in this book. If any such acknowledgment has been inadvertently omitted or miscredited, receipt of such information would be appreciated.

"Temporary Home" written by Zac Malloy, Luke Laird, and Carrie Underwood. Lyrics © BMG Rights Management, Universal Music Publishing Group, Sony/ATV Music Publishing LLC. Lyrics Licensed & Provided by *LyricFind*.

Scripture quotations marked (ESV) are taken from the *Holy Bible, English Standard Version*. Copyright © 2001 by Crossway Bibles, a division of Good News Publishers. Used by permission. All rights reserved.

Scripture quotations marked (KJV) are taken from the *King James Version of the Bible*.

Scripture quotations marked (NIV) are taken from *The Holy Bible, New International Version*. Copyright © 1973, 1978, 1984, 2011 by Biblica, Inc. Used by permission of Zondervan. All rights reserved worldwide. zondervan.com

Scripture quotations marked (NLT) are from the *Holy Bible, New Living Translation*. Copyright © 1996, 2004, 2007 by Tyndale House Foundation. Used by permission of Tyndale House Publishers Inc., Carol Stream, Illinois. All rights reserved.

Cover design by Pamela Walker, W Design Studio
Interior design by Pamela Walker, W Design Studio
Cover photo by Dreamstime
Typeset by Aptara, Inc.

Printed and bound in the United States of America
10 9 8 7 6 5 4 3 2 1

*Do not conform to the pattern of this world, but be
transformed by the renewing of your mind.
Then you will be able to test and approve what
God's will is—his good, pleasing and perfect will.*

Romans 12:2 (NIV)

CONTENTS

INTRODUCTION

*But in these last days he has spoken to us by his Son,
whom he appointed heir of all things, and through
whom also he made the universe.*

Hebrews 1:2 (NIV)

When we think about how God works in our lives, we tend to think first of His healing or of the comfort or joy He provides. But if we look deeper at the effects of God's blessings, we begin to see that His work actually transforms our lives. And many times this transformation doesn't just affect ourselves, because one transformed life can transform the lives of others.

God tells us that all things are part of His plan. Romans 8:28 says "...God causes all things to work together for good to those who love God, to those who are called according to His purpose." (NASB)

In each story in *Transformed by Heaven,* you'll read how a near-death experience—a visit to heaven—dramatically changed lives. You'll discover how each of the people who witnessed the afterlife returned ready to carry out the message they received while in heaven, to make God's plan the center of their lives. And how their transformation, in turn, transformed those whose lives they touched.

We hope these stories of amazing heavenly encounters will help you think about God's transforming work in your life—in this life and as you anticipate the next.

On Being Transformed

By Ginger Rue

*There are no circumstances in your life where
God will not stand with you and help you,
no matter what the trouble may be.*

Norman Vincent Peale

In one of T. S. Eliot's most famous works, "The Love Song of J. Alfred Prufrock," the poem's narrator is a lonely older man who longs for female companionship. J. Alfred Prufrock struggles with self-doubt and insecurity and fears even talking to women—he's terrified that if he opens his mouth to speak, foolish or boring words will come tumbling out.

How he wishes he had something interesting to say, something that would capture a listener's attention! At one point in the poem, Prufrock muses about how different things could be if only he could share something extraordinary...something like...

"I am Lazarus, come from the dead/Come back to tell you all, I shall tell you all..."

Certainly, that would do the trick.

Who wouldn't hang on Lazarus's every word? Who wouldn't want to know every detail of what Lazarus saw and heard and felt after being dead and buried for four days?

And yet, the real Lazarus—the one with such an enthralling story to tell—utters not a single word. Not in any of the four Gospel accounts.

Certain Death, Certain Life

You're about to read a book about extraordinary encounters. Millions of people are fascinated by stories that offer a glimpse into the hereafter, especially when those glimpses are accompanied by visions of peace and perfect love. Even so, what we call near-death experiences are controversial in the Christian community. Some believe wholeheartedly the stories they hear from those who have nearly crossed over into death, while others dismiss these tales as simply "hocus pocus"[1] or point out that the content of near-death experiences apparently differs across cultural and religious lines.[2] Nevertheless, minister Randy Frazee, author of *What Happens after You Die,* pinpoints the appeal of near-death experience stories: "We so want them to be true."[3]

> *Millions of people are fascinated by stories that offer a glimpse into the hereafter.*

As Frazee explains, "On one end of the spectrum, people cling to these stories to give them the evidence they need that there is more to this life. Others vehemently criticize the experience for a variety of reasons, from medical to theological."[4] Skeptics based on theology point out that there is no need for any further information about life after death: the "evidence [we] need that there is more to this life," as Frazee puts it, is already given to us in the Holy Bible. Jesus has already told us what to expect after we die, and we know that His testimony is trustworthy. Instead of giving us Lazarus's firsthand account, the Bible gives us the words of Christ. For who is greater—the one who is raised from the dead, or the One who raises him?

The only person with more knowledge than Lazarus about the afterlife is Christ, the God of the living and the dead. Though Lazarus had experienced something most of us never will this side of heaven, whatever he had to say could not have been more important than what those around him would hear from Jesus. Instead of giving us words from Lazarus, the Bible devotes its attention to the Living Word Himself.

Lazarus died and would have stayed dead until judgment day had Christ not chosen to perform a miracle to reveal the power of God at that moment. Though He knew Lazarus was sick, Jesus waited two more days before traveling to Bethany, where, by the time He arrived, Lazarus's lifeless body lay in a tomb. His sisters, Mary and Martha, knowing that Jesus had power over life and death, both remarked, "Lord, if you had been here, my brother would not have died." (John 11: 21, 32 NIV) And when Jesus asked for the stone to be moved away from the tomb's entrance, the ever-practical Martha reminded the Lord about the stench of decaying flesh. This timeline of events clearly shows us that what Lazarus had was most definitely not a *near*-death experience, making what Jesus did for him most definitely a miracle that proved to everyone who witnessed it that Jesus was indeed the Son of God.

The story of Lazarus being raised from the dead was so overwhelming that it was the last straw for the religious leaders of Jesus's day. "If we let him go on like this, everyone will believe in him," the chief priests

and the Pharisees of the Sanhedrin fretted at a strategy meeting following Lazarus's return. (John 11:48, NIV) The Gospel of John tells us that
"from that day on they plotted to take [Jesus's] life." (John 11:53, NIV)

Of course, their idea of damage control after Lazarus's story got out
resulted in an even bigger conspiracy when Jesus Himself arose from
the dead. Like Lazarus, Jesus spent enough days in the tomb so that
there was no mistake about His spirit
having left His body, even though non-
believers have since scrambled to offer
the "swooning" theory (the idea that
Jesus didn't actually die on the cross, but
passed out for a time) as a way to discredit
the Resurrection. The religious leaders of the day conspired with the
Romans to craft a narrative that the soldiers guarding the tomb had
fallen asleep and that the disciples had stolen Jesus's body. Never mind
the fact that falling asleep on the job meant certain execution for
Roman soldiers, or that this theory gives way too much credit to the
then-scattered, terrified, ragtag group of disciples. The "official" story
to this day is that the most powerful government in the ancient world
couldn't manage to keep track of one dead body that they had every
incentive to guard with all they had.

One thing we can take away from the resurrection of both Lazarus
and Jesus Himself is that when God chooses to show His power, He
does so in spectacular fashion. And when He wants us to know something, He makes sure to get His message across clearly.

So what are we to think, then, about people who flatline or lose brain
activity for a time before being revived? These are stories not of people

> *When God chooses
> to show His power, He
> does so in spectacular
> fashion.*

who have already been buried, but who nonetheless for a short time might have been considered dead. Can we count on their testimony of what they tell us they saw? Should we look to them for wisdom about how to live before we die?

A Dead Man's Wish and the Desire of the Living

In Luke 16: 27–31 (NIV), Jesus tells of a rich man and another Lazarus (not the one He raised from the dead). In this story, the selfish, rich man dies and goes to a place of torment, while the soul of the good yet poor man Lazarus goes to the bosom of Abraham and finds comfort. Filled with regret at how he has wasted his own life and squandered his chance at redemption, the rich man begs Father Abraham to send Lazarus back to earth to warn his brothers about the torment awaiting them after death:

> "I beg you, father, send Lazarus to my family, for I have five brothers. Let him warn them, so that they will not also come to this place of torment."
>
> Abraham replied, "They have Moses and the Prophets; let them listen to them."
>
> "No, father Abraham," he said, "but if someone from the dead goes to them, they will repent."
>
> He said to him, "If they do not listen to Moses and the Prophets, they will not be convinced even if someone rises from the dead."

Some scholars believe this is not, in fact, a parable but rather a true story, pointing to the fact that Jesus uses the name of a specific person, which He does not do in any of His parables.[5] Whether fact or parable, perhaps the point was not so much to give information about the afterlife as to foreshadow Jesus's own death and resurrection. He knew that there would be some who would never believe in Him, even after He rose from the dead. And yet, the story shows that Jesus understood the human desire to know about what happens when we die and how most of us would be eager to receive a message from beyond the grave.

> *Those of us who love Jesus and long to be with Him hunger for a glimmer of glory.*

This takes us back to Frazee's point: *we so want to believe.* Those of us who love Jesus and long to be with Him hunger for any glimmer of glory we can get. And indeed, some stories of beyond do align with scriptural teachings, such as the story young Kennedy Buettner told his parents after his father, a physician, performed CPR on what his medical training told him was Kennedy's dead body. Like the Bereans described in Acts 17:11, Dr. and Mrs. Buettner listened to Kennedy's story "with all eagerness, examining the Scriptures daily to see if these things were so." They accepted Kennedy's words not only because they knew he was too young and innocent to know how to concoct a near-death experience story but also because what he said did not violate what they knew to be the infallible Word of God.

Beyond Curiosity

Beyond our hunger for more knowledge about the afterlife, stories of near-death experiences also appeal to us because of how they change people. Many near-death experiencers say that they return to

earth with a newfound sense of peace and comfort, and that the concerns of this life seem inconsequential in comparison to what they have
witnessed. Again, this type of wisdom and centeredness is something all
Christians long for—or should. Regardless of our individual theological positions on the validity of near-death experiences, how glorious that
any of us, whether we've come close to death or not, can be personally
transformed by God! The Bible is filled with examples of encounters
with Jesus that changed those touched by Him forever. From simple
but profound words spoken to the woman at the well to more (literally)
earthshaking phenomena, such as the rending of the temple veil after
Jesus surrendered His Spirit at Calvary, a true brush with Jesus leaves
us with no choice but to declare, "'Truly, this [is] the Son of God!'"
(Matthew 27:54, ESV)

Persecutor to Persecuted

Saul of Tarsus was not somebody you'd want to get on the wrong
side of in ancient Jerusalem. When we first meet Saul in Acts 8,
he is giving his full approval to the stoning of Stephen, who has just
powerfully proclaimed Jesus as the Messiah. Our first glimpse of Saul
is as a young man guarding the coats of those who didn't want to soil
their clothing during the brutal and vicious work of stoning someone.
We soon learn that this same Saul is a leading force behind the "great
wave of persecution" against Christians: Saul was "going everywhere to
destroy the church. He went from house to house, dragging out both
men and women to throw them into prison." (Acts 8:3, NLT)

Saul had a passion for his work, and he had every reason to be proud
of his pedigree. He was "a pure-blooded citizen of Israel and a member

of the tribe of Benjamin—a real Hebrew if there ever was one! [He] was a member of the Pharisees, who demand[ed] the strictest obedience to the Jewish law. [He] was so zealous that [he] harshly persecuted the church. And as for righteousness, [he] obeyed the law without fault."

> *But then Saul saw the light—a light so powerful it knocked him to the ground.*

(Philippians 3:5-6, NLT) He didn't think of persecuting Christians as simply his duty, though. He "was eager to kill the Lord's followers." (Acts 9:1, NLT) Perhaps as he traveled the road to Damascus with letters granting him the authority to imprison Christian men and women, he may have been relishing the thought of bringing them "back to Jerusalem in chains." (Acts 9:2, NLT)

But then Saul saw the light—a light so powerful it knocked him to the ground and left him blind. And he heard the voice of Jesus.

Suddenly, the man so zealous to persecute Christians had a new calling—and a new identity in Christ as the Apostle Paul.

The man who once listed his credentials as a Pharisee among Pharisees developed an even more impressive resume as an apostle. His zeal for destroying Christianity paled in comparison to his willingness to suffer anything in order to preach about the risen Savior. Saul the persecutor became Paul the persecuted. In 2 Corinthians 11:24-27 (NIV), Paul enumerates his sufferings as an apostle of Christ:

Five times I received from the Jews the forty lashes minus one. Three times I was beaten with rods, once I was pelted with stones, three times I was shipwrecked, I spent a night and a day in the open sea, I have been constantly on the move. I have been in danger from rivers, in danger from bandits, in danger from my fellow Jews, in danger from Gentiles; in danger in the city, in danger in the country, in danger at sea; and in danger from false believers. I have labored and toiled and have often gone without sleep; I have known hunger and thirst and have often gone without food; I have been cold and naked.

And how did Paul feel about the hardships he faced? He considered them "not worthy to be compared with the glory which shall be revealed in us." (Romans 8:18, KJV) Although the Bible does not tell us how Paul died, it is believed that the Emperor Nero had him beheaded for his Christian faith.[6] Saul to Paul is an astonishing transformation, but only one example of the power of an encounter with Christ.

Thunderous to Loving

Jesus nicknamed the apostles John and his brother James "Sons of Thunder" in Mark 3:17, perhaps to indicate how bold or fiery they could be. We don't get to see much of their personalities in Gospels, but we do know that they wanted Jesus to call down fire from heaven to destroy a Samaritan village that did not welcome Jesus, and we know that Jesus rebuked them for this. (Luke 9: 51–55) Anyone who's ever struggled with a temper (that would be most all of us!), can certainly relate to James and John. But walking with Jesus transformed John from an ambitious and judgmental man into a gentle and loving spirit. In fact, John is known as "the Apostle of Love." Jesus didn't necessarily take away John's boldness, but He did shape it into a form that served God. John was the only apostle who had the courage to stand at the foot of the cross, but he also had the kind of loving heart that Jesus wanted for His followers. After all, when Jesus chose someone to take care of His mother, He chose John. (John 19:25–27)

This "son of thunder" spent the rest of his life loving and caring for the early church, offering them encouragement in his letters (John 1, 2, and 3) and through his Revelation. His beautifully poetic Gospel account shows us how his zeal and his gentleness combined when in the first chapter he proclaims that Jesus is the Word that brought us light and that "the light shines in the darkness, and the darkness can never extinguish it." (John 1:5, NLT) The man who once had trouble controlling his righteous anger came to address the fledgling church as his "dear children" (1 John 2:1), urging them over and over to love one another.

John shows how the love of Jesus can transform our potentially negative traits into something useful for the Kingdom. Although John was extremely loving, the boldness Jesus originally noted in him remained. According to *Fox's Book of Martyrs*, John was sent to Rome, "where it is affirmed he was cast into a cauldron of boiling oil. He escaped by miracle, without injury." The only apostle not to have died for Christ, John nevertheless was willing to face what would have been certain death without divine intervention.

Stiff Neck to Camel Knees

While Jesus was the only begotten Son of God, He was not the only child of Mary. According to the Bible, Jesus had four half brothers and more than one half sister. (Matthew 13:55–56) Proving Jesus's statement that "a prophet is not dishonored, except in his hometown, and among his relatives, and in his household" (Mark 6:4, NASB), Jesus's brother James (not the same James who was a "son of thunder") did not at first believe that Jesus was the Messiah. In what was no doubt a bitter foretaste of what the Lord would soon experience at Calvary, James and the other brothers openly mock Jesus, and John 7:5 states plainly that "even his brothers didn't believe in him." How James managed to live among the Lord for a few decades and witness His miracles without seeing who He really was is pretty remarkable. It would take some

> *It would take some serious stubbornness to resist worshipping God when He is right in front of you.*

serious stubbornness to resist worshipping God when He is right in front of you, especially for that length of time. But somehow, James managed it.

When Jesus raised Himself from the dead, we are told that one of the people He appeared to was James. (1 Corinthians 15:7) Scholars are divided on which James the Bible refers to here, but what they do agree on is that James the brother of Jesus went on to become a great leader in the church. It makes sense that seeing the risen Savior could have this transformative effect on even the most stiff-necked unbeliever. James became a pillar in the early church, as described by Paul in Galatians 2:9. His eponymous epistle is full of practical wisdom for Christian living, including some of the strongest words in the Bible about controlling the tongue. One can only wonder whether James looked back ruefully on the words he'd used to mock Jesus when he warned his fellow Christians that "the tongue is a flame of fire...a whole world of wickedness." (James 3:6, NLT)

James's epistle also stresses the power of prayer: "The earnest prayer of a righteous person has great power and produces wonderful results."

(James 5:16, NLT) Historians indicate that James practiced what he preached. According to the account of a second-century Christian named Hegessipus,[7] James was called "Old Camel Knees" because the

> *No matter how long we resist, the power of Jesus is strong enough to change us completely.*

skin on his knees became so wrinkled from bowing before God in continual prayer. Kneeling to pray is physical manifestation of humility. Paul says in Philippians 2:10 (NIV) that "at the name of Jesus every knee should bow." How beautiful that the brother of our Lord, who once had no faith in Him, would go on to spend the rest of his life in humble submission. James shows us that no matter how long we resist, the power of Jesus is strong enough to change us completely.

Reed to Rock

Praise God that He sees our potential! When Jesus gave Simon the name "Peter," meaning "rock," it wasn't because Simon was there yet—but Jesus knew he would get there eventually.

Even though we don't like to admit it, most of us can identify all too well with who Peter was before Christ's crucifixion. "Even if everyone else deserts you, I will never desert you," Peter declares boldly in Matthew 26:33 (NLT). Shortly thereafter, as Jesus had said, Peter has denied three times that he even knows the Lord. Imagine the look on the Lord's face when He looks at Peter. No wonder "Peter went out, and wept bitterly." (Luke 22:62, KJV) Many of us who love Jesus have felt similar shame and regret when we ourselves have disappointed Him. Godly repentance, as Peter's life shows us, is a powerful tool for the Kingdom.

Like many of us, Peter struggled with guilt and shame; it was difficult for him to let go of his failure. Perhaps that's why the resurrected Christ asked him three times, "Do you love me?" (John 21)—a chance to symbolically "undo" the three denials. Peter's story shows us that God never gives up on us, that He wants to transform us into the person He knows we can be through His power.

Despite Peter's bold words that he would never deny Christ, he bent like a reed in the wind that day. But that day did not define the rest of Peter's life. Peter did, indeed, become the rock Jesus called him to be. It was Peter who first preached the risen Savior at Pentecost, Peter who defied the high priests who had warned him to stop preaching Christ: "We must obey God rather than any human authority," Peter courageously declares in Acts 5:29 (NLT). Imprisonment and beatings could not stop him. History tells us that the man who was once afraid to admit he knew Jesus would die for Him: "Peter is supposed to have suffered martyrdom at Rome, during the reign of the emperor Nero, being crucified with his head downward, at his own request" (*Fox's Book of Martyrs*). It has been said that Peter requested that his crucifixion be different than that of Jesus because he did not feel worthy to die the same death as his Savior.

What about Us?

The men mentioned here are just a small sampling of people in Scripture who were completely changed as the result of encountering Jesus. Our response to Jesus must be transformative as well. It's not merely a suggestion, but a command: "And be not conformed to this world: but be ye transformed by the renewing of your mind, that ye may prove what is that good, and acceptable, and perfect, will of God." (Romans 12:2, KJV)

Following Jesus should completely change how we think and how we act. If it doesn't, we aren't doing it right. While the stories in this book can be powerful and direct our thinking toward what awaits our eternal soul, a near-death experience is not required for us to be transformed by the gospel: "The death, burial, and resurrection of Christ is the only death experience we need to evoke a change within us."[8]

The Word itself is the greatest transformational entity known to mankind. Hebrews 4:12 (NASB) tells us that "the Word of God is living and powerful, and sharper than any two-edged sword, even penetrating as far as the division of soul and spirit, of both joints and marrow, and able to judge the thoughts and intentions of the heart." It has the power to change us into who God calls us to be. Today, whether or not we come close to tasting death before our time, the Word of God can and will transform us if we let it.

1 Miller, Dave. "What about 'Out-of-Body Experiences'?" http://apologeticspress.org/apPubPage.aspx?pub=1&issue=1125

2, 5, 8 McCown, Scott. "Thinking about Near Death Experiences." https://scottmccown.com/2020/10/15/thinking-about-near-death-experiences/

3, 4 Frazee, Randy. "What About Life-After-Death and Near-Death Experiences?" https://www.faithgateway.com/what-about-life-after-death-and-near-death-experiences/#.X3zuoFl7nb6

6 *Fox's Book of Martyrs.* https://www.gutenberg.org/files/22400/22400-h/22400-h.htm#Page_18

7 *The Memoirs of Hegessipus,* http://www.intratext.com/IXT/ENG0833/_P1T.HTM

The Simple Truth of Heaven

By Craig and Amy Buettner, as told to Ginger Rue

But in your hearts revere Christ as Lord. Always be prepared to give an answer to everyone who asks you to give the reason for the hope that you have. But do this with gentleness and respect.

1 Peter 3:15 (NIV)

By June 2000, the Buettner family was well into their spring and summer baseball routine. Craig, a family doctor and sports medicine specialist, and his wife, Amy, a stay-at-home mom, were the proud parents of five beautiful children: ten-year-old Jacob, five-year-old Hayden, four-year-old Kennedy ("KeKe" to his mom), two-year-old Isabelle, and six-week-old Markie. Markie had been named for his uncle Mark, Amy's brother, who had died tragically from a brain tumor less than a year before. Amy and her brother had been extremely close all their lives, and the entire family missed Mark terribly. Yet because of their deep and abiding faith in Jesus Christ, the Buettners held fast to their hope of seeing Mark again in heaven one day. They never wavered in their belief that that day would come.

Even still, no one expected four-year-old Kennedy to see Mark so soon.

Following is the astonishing true story of Kennedy Buettner and what happened when he was four years old, including his near-death experience, as told through the eyes of his parents.

The Boys of Summer
Craig

I was the assistant coach for Jacob's Little League baseball team, the Cubs. The boys had played hard that day but still lost, so as the unofficial team doctor, I prescribed a healthy dose of fun to revive their spirits. We all headed over to the home of one of the players whose family had a swimming pool. The kids could hardly wait to swim, and the adults could hardly wait to grill out and relax while the children had fun.

Amy

Relaxation? I wasn't sure I remembered what that word meant anymore! But getting all five kids, including Isabelle—who was still in a stroller—and Markie—who was still nursing—to the baseball field was just part of the routine. I'd always wanted five children, and I thrived in what I now look back on as "diaper bag mode."

I thrived in what I now look back on as "diaper bag mode."

Once I got everyone back into the car and we headed out for the party, I looked in the rearview mirror and saw KeKe touching the baby's face. Just before we'd left the ballpark, he and the other boys had been playing with a turtle they'd found. When I scolded Kennedy about touching the baby with "turtle hands," his little eyes grew wide as he looked to make sure his hands had not transformed into scaly paws! I tried to explain about germs and washing our hands before we touched the baby, but to be honest, I was hot, tired, and hungry, and after rounding everyone up and breaking down the stroller, I was probably not my most patient.

When we got to the Dockerys' house for the pool party, I could hardly wait to sit down and have a juicy hamburger with fresh, home-grown tomatoes from their garden. I had plenty of help with the baby since everyone wanted to take turns holding him, and Isabelle was finally settled down too. Just as I was about to take that first bite into my hamburger, I felt a sudden urgency that pulled me to my feet:

Go find Kennedy.

I'd spoken with KeKe again just moments before we'd all gathered to bless the food. He'd asked if he would get to swim some more, and I'd assured him there would be more swimming after lunch. But after that brief conversation, where had he gone?

I scanned the pool, looking for Kennedy's little red swimsuit, but I saw nothing. Then I worried that he might have gone out front, so I checked to make sure he wasn't out there playing in the street. No sign of him.

I went to get Craig.

Craig

I could see the urgency in Amy's eyes. Just as she had done, I checked the pool first. Nothing. I asked the other kids if they'd seen him; they hadn't. I checked all over the house to see if he'd found a toy to play with inside. Still no sign of him.

That's when I heard Jacob's voice: "Daddy! Daddy! We found Kennedy at the bottom of the pool!"

A Parent's Nightmare
Craig

I hadn't really panicked up until that point, but suddenly terror consumed me. Jacob and his friends had caught a glimpse of red at the bottom of the pool and had gone to investigate. Once they'd realized it was a person, without missing a beat, the boys had jumped in and pulled Kennedy from the pool. At first, Jacob didn't even realize the bloated blob the boys pulled out of the water was his brother. Kennedy's body was gray from a lack of oxygen in his bloodstream, and his abdomen was swollen with water. As the boys dragged him to the side of the pool, his body flopped around like a rag doll. His skin was cold. His pupils were fixed and dilated, and he was completely unresponsive. Jacob had recognized Kennedy only by his long eyelashes. That's when he ran to find me.

> *Kennedy's body was gray, and his abdomen was swollen with water.*

My medical training immediately kicked in, overcoming my fear as Kennedy's father. I began performing CPR on what was obviously a dead body. As I pumped Kennedy's chest trying to restart his heart, I felt hands on my back as the team's head coach and other men prayed over me and quoted scripture while begging God for my son's life. At some point, I looked up and shouted, "You are not going to die!" But for a full five minutes, I still couldn't get a heartbeat or any response at all. Finally, Kennedy drew a breath, and a little color returned to his body. The EMTs arrived about seven minutes later. I never stopped doing CPR until they took over. He had taken one breath, but he wasn't breathing, wasn't stable. The whole time, I was going over different medical scenarios and possible courses of action in my mind.

During those twelve horrible minutes, I was in full "doctor mode." I couldn't stop long enough to comprehend what was happening to me as a father and a husband. But then, a sound come out of my wife that brought me into our terrible reality as parents.

Amy

I guess you'd call it a wail, a primal sound from the depths of my very soul. Things were coming out of my mouth that I had no control over. It was almost like I was having an out-of-body experience. Everything around me seemed to be covered in smoke. As Craig performed CPR, I held on to Kennedy's legs; they felt like rubber. At some point, I walked over to the fence and buried my head in my hands as I cried out to God: "Please, God. God, please, please, please."

Only weeks before, an elderly lady of great faith had told me to thank God during difficult times. Her words came rushing back to me in that moment, and I kept repeating, "Thank You, God. Thank You, God, for this. Thank You for what You are doing. Thank You for this." It sounds strange, I know...but those were the words I spoke.

Craig

I was so relieved when the EMTs arrived with their equipment. They were able to determine that Kennedy's oxygen saturation was 92 percent, a good number, and that his heart rhythm was normal. However, he was incoherent and innately fighting them as they were trying to place the tube, and he was unresponsive to commands of any kind. Not good signs. He was pale and still somewhat bloated, and I saw signs of hypoxia (low oxygen) to his brain—involuntary motions in his extremities, besides spasms and contractions. His back was arched and his face was tight.

> *We both knew that Kennedy was on the brink of death.*

As they loaded Kennedy into the ambulance to take him to the local hospital, Amy and I followed behind. She was throwing up the whole time.

At the hospital, Kennedy began posturing, a medical term meaning he was involuntarily flexing and extending his arms and legs. Posturing is a sign of severe brain injury. I knew this from my medical background, but Amy knew it too—she'd seen her brother, Mark, posture before he died. We both knew it was a sign that Kennedy was on the brink of death.

Amy

All of these doctors and nurses were standing around my son, and I remember thinking, "This room is full of health-care professionals, and not one of them can save my child." It was at that moment I put my hands on top of KeKe and began praying out loud: "Dear Lord, You are the true Physician! No one else can save my son! Only You can heal him!"

Craig

As the doctors continued their evaluation, Amy and I stood at Kennedy's bedside the entire time. I think we were allowed in the trauma bay because of my relationship with the doctors working on Kennedy and the fact that they did not expect him to live. Because of the posturing, Amy and I both knew that he still was not getting enough oxygen to his brain. It seemed that Kennedy was unaware of his surroundings, so the doctors tried to spread out the frequency of his sedatives to allow him to wake up, but without the sedatives, he thrashed and screamed incoherently and continued to posture. Perhaps even worse, the water from the pool had caused his lungs to swell, creating a pulmonary edema, which makes it difficult to breathe because the oxygen can't flow into the lung tissue. The swelling was only getting worse. None of his test results were encouraging.

The ventilator they put Kennedy on wasn't able to deliver the appropriate pressure to push oxygen into his lungs. In normal circumstances, the ventilator at our local hospital would have been fine, but when the X-ray came back showing such severe swelling and the blood gases test showed such a low oxygen level, the doctors knew Kennedy needed a ventilator with extra pressure to force the oxygen into his bloodstream.

Within only about thirty minutes of Kennedy's arrival at the local hospital, the decision was made to fly Kennedy by helicopter to Children's Hospital in Birmingham, an hour away, where he could be put on a specialized ventilator. It was his only shot. Otherwise, he wouldn't last through the night. We couldn't go in the helicopter with him. Friends drove us to Birmingham, along with Markie, since he was still nursing. Other friends took care of our other children until Amy's parents could make the seven-hour trip from their home to take over. My parents drove to Birmingham to meet Amy and me at the hospital to provide support and to help with Markie.

Driving to Birmingham was the longest drive of our lives. One of the friends driving us was a neurologist who went to our church. Amy peppered him with questions the whole time, and he kept telling her stories of patients of his who had survived against all odds. The entire time, though, I worried not so much that Kennedy would die, but that he would live...with the consequences of my actions. I knew there was little hope that Kennedy would survive without severe brain damage. Had I saved my son's life so that he could live the rest of his years in a vegetative state? Was that the kind of life he would want for himself? Would I have shown greater mercy by allowing my son to die?

> *I wondered if I had saved my son's life so that he could live the rest of his years in a vegetative state.*

Amy

I was worried, of course, but also racked with guilt. The enemy knows exactly where to hit each of us in our weakest spots.

For me, the fact that I'd scolded Kennedy about his "turtle hands" ate me alive. Oh, how could I have used such a sharp tone with my beautiful little boy? I remembered also how he'd casually asked me if he could get back in the pool after lunch. I'd replied, "Sure, after we eat." But I'd never said, "Do not go to the pool without me." And I'd never explicitly explained that the rope across the pool divided the shallow end from the deep end. I berated myself for these oversights. If only I could go back and do everything right. If only I could have another chance to say the things I should have said.

KeKe was already in the ICU at Children's before we were even out of Tuscaloosa. When we arrived at the hospital an hour later, we were put in a conference room to wait on the doctors to come talk to us. We sat in that room for at least an hour, maybe two. We were told they would come get us when they were finished, so Craig did not try to go into the ICU. Instead, he stayed with me—both of us alternating between pacing, praying, crying, or staring off into space. We talked in general terms of our fears and hopes, but Craig never told me his concerns about Kennedy surviving with severe brain damage. He chose to bear that burden alone so as not to give me any more fears than I already had. Instead, we comforted each other as best we could. At one point, when I was overcome with terror that Kennedy would die, Craig held me and reminded me that if the Lord took Kennedy, Mark would be there.

During that time, the medical staff did different procedures for Kennedy, including replacing IV lines, putting in an arterial line to monitor his blood pressure and other vital signs, and placing him on the ventilator that could give him pressure to keep his lungs open. It took them a long time to get the vent settings just right in order to stabilize him. To accomplish all this, they had to paralyze him with medications. Finally, the main physician, Dr. Buckmaster, came in to talk to us. Maybe because Craig was a doctor too, or maybe because he was just a straight shooter, Dr. Buckmaster didn't sugarcoat things.

"I have another similar case right now," he said. "Another drowning patient. It's been two weeks, and he's still on the ventilator, unconscious. If and when Kennedy comes to, he probably won't recognize you for some time."

"How long?" I asked.

"There's no way to predict," he replied. "You should be ready for the long haul. In addition to the initial dangers he's already faced, there are other dangers that come the longer he's in the hospital. We'll be watching for those issues. But I want you both to keep in mind that this will take a long time to resolve. Kennedy is a very sick little boy."

After Dr. Buckmaster finished speaking with us, the nurse came and took us to the ICU.

Craig

To be honest, when I first saw Kennedy in the ICU at Children's, I was just relieved to see him alive. From what I had seen on the edge of the pool and then the way he'd been posturing at the other hospital, this was a huge improvement. Who would've ever thought I'd be so happy to see my little boy with a tube down his throat, an arterial line in his groin, an IV in his arm, and four-point restraints holding him down? But in that moment, it was a welcome sight.

> It gave me some comfort to see that my boy was literally covered in scripture.

Amy

While Craig and I tried to absorb the gravity of the situation, friends and family began arriving at the hospital. Many wrote Bible verses on cards and gave them to me. Not sure what to do with all these pieces of paper, I finally decided to tape them all over KeKe's bed. It gave me some comfort to see that my boy was literally covered in scripture.

I still had no idea what Craig was going through, worrying about Kennedy not being whole again. Ignorance was a certain form of bliss. I didn't understand how low the chances of his full recovery truly were. The doctors talked about brain damage, but I couldn't really process it; all I cared about was KeKe's survival. I prayed, "Lord, I will take him any way You will give him back to me."

Children's Hospital has some rooms available for families of patients, and one room down the hall from Kennedy became open the next day. If it hadn't, I don't know how I would've been able to nurse Markie because there was no way I could leave Kennedy in the hospital. Craig and I had to take turns sitting with him because only one family member at a time was allowed. During Craig's time, I nursed Markie in the room the hospital provided for us, and during my turn, if Craig didn't have the baby, friends and family cared for Markie in the waiting room. The only reason I left KeKe's side was to nurse the baby.

Exhausted as I was from worry and nursing, I could hardly sleep. In the ICU room, there was only a chair, so I couldn't lie down. When I would finally collapse back in the room they gave Craig and me, I would envision Kennedy deep underwater, thrashing about and struggling, as all the while the water's surface was deceptively silent and still. I would hear him under that water, calling for me.

This went on for three days while Keke lay comatose in the hospital. On that third day, a Saturday, I finally fell into a deep sleep I could no longer fight. But almost as soon as sleep overtook me, I bolted upright, consumed with fear, almost paralyzed. I just knew that something terrible had happened while I was asleep. I ran down the hall to Kennedy, but when I looked around, nothing had changed. In fact, Kennedy was lying peacefully in the hospital bed. I looked at the scriptures all over his bed and decided to take out my Bible, hoping to find some comfort.

I hardly knew where to start. I remember thinking, "Today is June 18, so I will read Psalm 18." When I did, the words astounded me:

> He reached down from on high and took hold of me;
>> he drew me out of deep waters.
> He rescued me from my powerful enemy,
>> from my foes, who were too strong for me.
> They confronted me in the day of my disaster,
>> but the LORD was my support.
> He brought me out into a spacious place;
>> he rescued me because he delighted in me.

The words spoke directly to my heart and to my fears of KeKe not returning to us whole. Of course God would rescue Kennedy because He delighted in him! This precious child never failed to bring joy and laughter wherever he went. This was my silly boy who, when asked in Sunday school to name something God had made, had stood up, dropped his pants, and announced "God made my booty!"

"Kennedy is going to be healed! And something really big is going to happen!"

With the words from that psalm, God had reached down and taken hold of me. The doctor came in later that morning and told me that KeKe was not even close to being able to come off the ventilator, but I knew deep in my heart that he was going to be okay. I ran back to our room where Craig was waiting. Instead of telling him what the doctor said, I told him, "Kennedy is going to be healed! And not just healed—something really big is going to happen!" Craig tried to share my conviction, but deep inside, he was still wrestling with fear and guilt.

A Hopeful Sign
Craig

Like I said before, I somehow knew that Kennedy wasn't going to die, so that wasn't my fear. What concerned me was what kind of life my son would live from then on. I feared that I'd sentenced him to life as a vegetable. I pictured him watching his brothers and sister jump and play while he lay unable to move, unable to ever fully live life. And I would always be the one who'd caused it. I was relieved to see Amy's change in demeanor—I could see the "peace that passes all understanding" all over her face, and I knew it was real. She spoke with such confidence and surety.

As for me, I felt that I knew too much based on my medical background. It wasn't just about Kennedy surviving; it was about his being whole. Amy was certain that not only would Kennedy live, but that he would be completely healed. And at that point, I just couldn't buy into that kind of hope. I wanted to. I read my Bible. I prayed. I tried to take comfort offered from visiting friends. But nothing eased my mind. I was still depending more on my experience as a physician than on my faith in Jesus.

On the fourth day of Kennedy's hospitalization, the doctors began to wean him off the drugs that were sedating him. Because he hadn't thrashed or tried to remove any of his tubes, they had removed his restraints, freeing his arms and legs. Amy and I could touch him, but he still had a lot of lines going in, besides the ventilator, so we could only hold his hand. When he woke up, we knew he wouldn't be able to talk because he was still on the ventilator, but we needed to find out if he could communicate nonverbally.

Kennedy was so unexplainably peaceful and relaxed. He never seemed fearful, frustrated, tearful, or negative.

When the neurologist and I asked him yes or no questions, Kennedy shook or nodded his head appropriately in response. This was encouraging—and to be honest, strange. He was so unexplainably peaceful and relaxed. He never seemed fearful, frustrated, tearful, or negative at any point. Some of the nurses commented about how unusual his response to the situation was. He was calm even when Amy or I would have to leave the room for the nursing shift change.

The neurologist was as taken aback by Kennedy's demeanor as I was. He told me, "I've never cleared anyone to be discharged while they were still on the vent, but I'm coming pretty close with him." Obviously, he was joking somewhat because a ventilator is a pretty serious piece of medical equipment, but beyond that, he couldn't see anything else that Kennedy physically needed.

Even so, brain damage was still not yet ruled out. The consequences from the amount of time Kennedy's brain was without oxygen might not become apparent for years.

When the neurologist left and I was alone in the room with Kennedy, I asked him if he wanted to watch some cartoons. He nodded. I tuned the television to a local station that was playing cartoons.

Kennedy began shaking his head, for the first time seeming slightly agitated.

"What's wrong, buddy?" I asked.

He held up both of his hands, all fingers up but thumbs turned in. I stared at him for a moment. "Four?" I said. "Four, four?"

Kennedy nodded.

Four, four...Forty-four!

That was the channel on our home television for Cartoon Network!

How could a four-year-old who was supposed to be brain-dead remember his favorite TV station? He couldn't—that's how. My heart sang, *There's nothing wrong with my little man's brain!*

When I turned the station to Cartoon Network, Kennedy tried to laugh at the show, but the ventilator tube caused him to gag and choke. He just pointed at the tube, smiled, and rolled his eyes.

I tried to let relief wash over me, but I couldn't dismiss the fact that Kennedy was still on a ventilator, relying on it to pump oxygen into his lungs so that he could stay alive. The pulmonologist had said the ventilator would have to stay in for several more days at least and that Kennedy's organs might be permanently damaged. He wasn't out of the woods yet.

I ran through all the medical what-ifs I knew from my training: What if he developed a hospital-acquired infection? What if he developed a blood clot in his leg from lying immobile for so long? What if that blood clot traveled to his lungs? What if his lungs became so swollen that antibiotics couldn't help? What if he had a reaction to the antibiotics? Any of these what-ifs could mean death. And even though his brain seemed well enough to remember a TV station, there was no guarantee that Kennedy would continue to develop physically, intellectually, or emotionally. My brain was in hyperdrive, and I felt completely powerless.

By the twentieth, five days since the accident, I knew I had to do something...but what?

I thought of Amy's example of reading Psalm 18 on the eighteenth. I decided to read Psalm 20 on the twentieth.

When I got to verses six and seven, I could feel the words speaking directly to me:

> Now this I know:
>> The LORD gives victory to his anointed.
>>> He answers him from his heavenly sanctuary
>>> with the victorious power of his right hand.
>> Some trust in chariots and some in horses,
>>> but we trust in the name of the LORD our God.

The victory would be the Lord's, not mine or any other physician's. I had not been the one who'd brought Kennedy back to life: God had done that. I had to put my trust in God, not in my own "chariots" or "horses." Kennedy's recovery was not in my hands, but in God's. I reminded myself that with God, all things are possible.

When it was Amy's turn to come back in, I immediately told her, "Kennedy's coming off the ventilator today!"

Kennedy's recovery was not in my hands, but in God's. I reminded myself that with God, all things are possible.

"The doctor said today?" she asked.

"No," I replied. "The doctor said he wouldn't be able to come off for several weeks. But it's today. I know it is."

Amy looked at me.

"It's not my medical opinion," I told her. "It's not a gut feeling. I just know."

My trust was no longer in medical expertise. My trust was now in the Great Physician.

Conviction of Things Not Seen
Amy

The team of doctors agreed to take Kennedy off the ventilator that day, with the caveat that if it did not go well, they would have to paralyze him and replace the tube. The lead doctor was skeptical, but Craig had this unshakeable confidence that it would work. Craig understood all the medical things I didn't—he knew all about the vent settings, the lab values, the X-ray results—but none of that fazed him. His trust was in the Lord. Craig was eerily calm when the moment came to remove the tube. He knew it would work. The tube would come out, and KeKe would breathe on his own.

It was such a big moment to have gone by so quickly, but all of a sudden, the tube was out.

Kennedy coughed and gagged, and it's possible my own heart may have stopped until his chest stopped heaving and began rising and falling in gentle pulses. Next, they removed all the other lines except for one IV.

"Would you like to hold your son?" the nurse asked me. She gestured for me to sit in a rocking chair.

When they put KeKe in my arms, he had that sterile hospital smell, but I inhaled the scent deeply, savoring it, as though I were in the sweetest flower garden. Feeling him in my embrace again, all I could do was kiss his sweet face over and over and over.

An Amazing Journey

Amy

As I held my little boy close, I could finally ask him the question that had been tormenting Craig and me: How had he ended up in the pool? He'd always been afraid to jump into the water unless his daddy was less than three feet away. How could he have wound up at the deep end, nine feet down? Had he slipped and hit his head? Had he been trying to reach a toy? Was he trying to swim in the deep end like he'd seen the bigger boys do? I had to know.

> *"Mommy," he said.*
> *"I flew through clouds.*
> *I flew through walls,*
> *and I flew through you!"*

"Little buddy," I said. "You were asleep for a long time. What happened? How did you end up in the pool?"

But Keke seemed to ignore the last question, focusing only on telling me what had happened to him.

"Mommy," he said. "I flew through clouds. I flew through walls, and I flew through you!"

At first, I thought he was trying to describe the water. But then I somehow realized that he was telling me something big.

Before Kennedy could say anything more, the doctor asked him if he needed anything.

KeKe replied in a raspy voice, "Hamburger."

Craig

Seeing Amy and Kennedy in that rocking chair was the second-most beautiful sight of the two of them I'd ever seen—second only to the sight of his birth.

I was overcome with joy, thinking of how our son had endured so much in the past few days—tied down to a bed with a machine breathing for him, separated from his whole family. But I knew he had never been separated from God. Soon, we would find out how true that really was.

They moved Kennedy out of the ICU to a room on the pulmonary floor, and we got Kennedy the hamburger he wanted. Before we let him dig in, we cautioned him about not choking. Then we watched as he nibbled it like a hungry little bird.

Although all his tests were encouraging, we knew his lungs had been damaged, and the pulmonologist said that Kennedy would still need another week in the hospital. That was fine with us. We had no complaints.

But then something happened.

Spiritual Warfare
Amy

Kennedy's new room had a roll-out bed instead of just a chair, so I would be able to sleep next to him that night while Craig stayed in the other room, taking care of the baby. The only light in Keke's hospital room came from the crack under the door, where the light from the hallway seeped in. Kennedy was hooked up to oxygen because without it, his oxygen levels were as low as 82 percent. Craig explained that normal was 92 percent, so the oxygen line needed to stay in. Still, compared to the ventilator, little prongs just inside his nostrils seemed such a small thing to help Keke as his lungs recovered. He didn't even seem to notice the nasal prongs or his IV as he slept soundly.

As I listened to Kennedy breathing softly and peacefully on his own, I snuggled into the coziness of my bed. Sleep overtook me almost immediately. I was just over six weeks postpartum, and the last few days had been a roller coaster of exhaustion followed by the sweet exhilaration of KeKe's recovery. I slept like I'd never slept before, until I suddenly bolted awake.

It was sometime in the early morning hours and was still dark. I awoke in a panic, overwhelmed with dread. Immediately, I began to pray, although I had no idea what I was praying for. Then I looked over at Kennedy, and what I saw paralyzed me with fear.

> What I saw paralyzed me with fear. An indistinct, faceless figure was floating over KeKe's head.

Hovering over my little boy was a shadow: an indistinct, faceless figure, floating above KeKe's head. A heavy, black darkness filled the room. I could feel its weight on my own body, pulling me down so that I could not move. Although I was physically paralyzed, inside, my heart seemed to be beating ninety miles an hour. I don't know if I cried out, but the figure suddenly seemed to turn its attention away from Kennedy onto me.

Before I could think, I acted. "I claim the shed blood of my Lord Jesus Christ!" I said aloud. "In the name of Jesus Christ, I rebuke you! Leave us! Get away from my son!"

The dark figure suddenly whooshed past me. For a moment, the light from the hallway was extinguished, and the room went black as the demon went out through the crack under the door. Then, just as quickly as the light had disappeared from under the door, it reappeared again.

Immediately, I felt the heaviness lifted from the room.

KeKe was still breathing peacefully. He had slept through the whole thing.

Craig

We'd been told that Kennedy would have to remain in the hospital for at least another week since he had to stay hooked up to the oxygen. But somewhere in the night, Kennedy's oxygen tube had come off. When that happens, an alarm is supposed to go off to alert the medical staff, but no alarm had sounded. The doctors discovered it when they came in to do their rounds the next morning. Remarkably, Kennedy's vitals were good. "I'm writing an order to discontinue the oxygen," the doctor said. "He doesn't seem to need it. You can take him home."

After Amy told me about the shadowy figure she had rebuked in the name of Jesus, I could only think that it had been a demon. I don't know if the demon had removed Kennedy's oxygen to try to harm him or if the oxygen had come off some other way, but I do believe that Amy's rebuking that demon allowed Kennedy to heal. I believe that the dark spirit fled that room because of the power of Jesus and that this allowed Kennedy's lungs to be whole again.

After one week at Children's Hospital, Kennedy was going home.

Home Again
Craig

Kennedy's brothers and sister were so relieved and overjoyed to have him back home. Once we settled back in, all Kennedy wanted was for me to throw him some balls for batting practice. With his still-swollen

> As if his physical recovery had not amazed us all enough, we were about to be even more astonished.

belly, he looked like a child from a famine-stricken country, and he ran like a staggering, newborn colt, but watching him run and play again was awesome! "If you want, I'll throw this plastic ball all day long, little buddy," I told him.

A week later, we went back to Children's for a checkup. The pulmonologist put the new X-rays up on the screen next to the old ones. "These changes should have taken at least a month," he said. "Has he been using the inhaler we prescribed to help clear his lungs?"

"Only once," I replied. "He actually has been squirting his brothers with it."

The doctor declared that no more follow-up appointments would be necessary. Kennedy was healed!

As if his physical recovery had not amazed us all enough, we were about to be even more astonished. Kennedy had much to share with us about what had happened to him when he'd been "asleep."

"Mommy, I saw Jesus."
Amy

We never pressed Kennedy about what he had meant when he said he'd flown through clouds, through walls, and through me. We were just so ecstatic that he was alive and whole and back home with us. But KeKe wanted to share something important with us; we could tell. Sometimes we'd just be driving down the road, and he would start saying things from his car seat; at other random times, he'd initiate conversations about what had happened to him.

One day, about a week after he got out of the hospital, I was making him a peanut butter and jelly sandwich. Out of nowhere, Kennedy announced, "Mommy, when you die, you'll be with Uncle Mark right after you die." I felt a chill crawl up my spine. It had been only about a year since my brother, Mark, had died from the brain tumor, and I missed him terribly. We all did. In the last few weeks of his life, I watched Mark deteriorate from the healthy, vibrant person he'd always been. I didn't want to press KeKe, so I just agreed with him.

Another day that same week, we were reading books in bed when Kennedy pointed at a family photograph that included Mark. The photo had been taken after his first brain surgery. Nonchalantly, KeKe said, "Uncle Mark doesn't have any more boo-boos on his head."

Over the next few weeks, Kennedy shared more and more. Calmly and matter-of-factly one day, out of nowhere, he told Craig and me that on the day of the accident, he was "going down in a whirlpool" and that an angel had picked him up. He said the angel picked him up and carried him, even though the angel did not have arms, and they flew. He said that at first, there was only one angel, but then there were "lots and lots of angels."

We let him keep talking without interrupting him. He said that when he and the angel stopped flying, he looked and saw a door on one side of him and a ladder on the other.

Whenever we asked him questions, he answered immediately. We could tell he wasn't trying to weave a story from his imagination. We didn't want to push too hard, and we didn't want to ask any leading questions. I gently asked him, "What else did you see?"

He repeated that the door was on his right and that something else was on his left.

"The angels you saw," I asked. "Were they happy or sad?"

I'll never forget the look on his face. It was complete disbelief that anyone could ask such a question. "They were happy!" he replied emphatically.

> *I'd never doubted that my brother was in heaven, but to hear it from my son thrilled my soul.*

I had been pondering in my heart the things KeKe had said previously about my brother, and finally, I just had to ask. "KeKe, did you see Uncle Mark?"

"Yes!" he exclaimed.

My heart leapt. "What did he look like?"

"They were both wearing all white. Uncle Mark looked just like Jesus! All his boo-boos were gone."

I'd never doubted that my brother was in heaven, but to hear it from my son thrilled my soul in a way I can never fully express.

I took two photographs of Mark—one from before the cancer had ravaged his body and one shortly before his death—and I showed them to Kennedy. "Which one did Uncle Mark look like?" I asked. Keke pointed to the pre-cancer photo that had been taken when Kennedy was less than two years old.

I had to fight back tears of joy. When Mark had been sick, I had prayed and prayed to God, asking Him to make Mark whole again. Now

I realized God had granted my request. My brother was whole, living with Jesus for eternity.

I quickly turned my attention back to KeKe, not wanting to lose this moment. He'd just told me that Mark looked like Jesus, so I asked, "And you saw Jesus?"

"Yes," he replied nonchalantly. It seemed to him a silly question. Why wouldn't he have seen Jesus? Then he described Jesus: He was dressed all in white, with a blue sash across His chest. Mark did not have to introduce them because they already knew each other. I thought about how Kennedy had said that Mark looked "just like Jesus." How could that be? I thought of the scripture in 1 Corinthians 15:49 (ESV): "And just as we have borne the image of the earthly man, so shall we bear the image of the heavenly man."

KeKe said they were standing on glass, and that the door he had seen to his right side was surrounded by jewels. He used that exact word: *jewels*. He had learned it from his brother Hayden, who'd learned it from a book. Before Kennedy's accident, the two of them had painted rocks and hidden them like buried treasure; then they'd encouraged their siblings to dig for their "jewels."

KeKe then went on to say that when they opened the door, "It was snowing in there." Then he stopped for a moment before returning to the subject of the ladder on his left that he'd mentioned. His voice got low, and I could tell he was filled with anxiety. Below that ladder, Kennedy said, "There was a volcano."

"Okay," I said. "Was the volcano part of heaven or was it someplace else, like separate?"

"Separate."

"Was there anything else there?" Craig asked.

"There were people in that volcano. And there was fire all around."

I tried not to show any emotion that might spook him when I asked, "Were those people happy or sad?"

"They were sad," KeKe replied. "There was a Pokemon in there with them."

"A Pokemon?" asked Craig.

"More like a dwagon," he said with his four-year-old's pronunciation.

"Were you scared, buddy?" I asked. "No, Daddy. I was with Jesus!"

"Was the dragon happy or was he sad?" I asked.

"He was *happy*," Kennedy said, obviously disturbed. "He looked at me and he smiled. Then he went, 'Grrrr!'"

Craig

Hearing Kennedy imitate that growl from the dragon sent a wave of cold over both Amy and me. "Were you scared, buddy?" I asked.

"No, Daddy. I was with Jesus!"

"What was that like?"

"I was standing on glass. I was invisible!"

Amy asked, "How did you get back?"

"Uncle Mark pushed me," he answered. "And an angel flew me back."

I could tell that Amy was having to fight to keep her voice from breaking when she asked, "Kennedy? Did your uncle Mark want to come with you?"

Kennedy looked up at his mother as if she were crazy.

"No!"

"Did you want to come back?"

Kennedy thought for a long time.

"Yes."

Searching for Answers
Craig

When Amy and I were alone, we prayed that we would be able to correctly process the things Kennedy had told us. We decided to dig deeper into God's Word for answers and seek wise counsel from strong Christians, including Amy's small-group Bible study leader and our minister.

Our pastor just happened to preach that Sunday on the parable of the rich man and Lazarus. Amy and I pondered over how similar it was to what Kennedy had told us about the separation between the people with Jesus and the people below with the "dwagon." Kennedy had not been taught that story in Bible class yet, nor had we taught it to him.

As we continued our study, we were led to Matthew 25:31–33. In this passage, we are told that "when the Son of Man comes in his glory," Jesus "will separate the people one from another as a shepherd separates the sheep from the goats. He will put the sheep on his right and the goats on his left." This, too, lined up with Kennedy's story: the door with the happy people was on the right, and the door with the volcano and the dragon was on the left, where the people were sad.

Kennedy had seen across that great chasm, and whether he was in heaven or some sort of edge between the two places is an interesting question, but—as Amy and I decided—it's one that is ultimately as pointless as wondering how Kennedy got to the bottom of that pool in the first place.

Amy

And as far as the dragon goes—the smiling Pokemon? We needed only to look to Revelation to corroborate KeKe's story. Revelation 12:9 describes how "the dragon was hurled down—that ancient serpent called the devil, or Satan, who leads the whole world astray." While Craig and I certainly think our boy is smart, we're pretty sure he hadn't been deciphering the book of Revelation at the age of four. And we're also pretty sure that he didn't just happen to make up a wild story that fits perfectly with the most prophetic book in the entire New Testament.

> *We're pretty sure that he didn't make up a wild story that fits perfectly with the most prophetic book in the New Testament.*

Even the details of his story align with scripture. Revelation 21:19–21 describes the foundations of the city walls of heaven as "decorated with every kind of precious stone" and "the great street of the city...as pure as transparent glass."

Every time I read that scripture, to this day, I can hear KeKe's little voice saying, "I was invisible. I was walking on glass."

The Right Focus
Craig

Kennedy was an amazing boy and today is an amazing young man. And while his story is powerful, we want to be clear: Kennedy is not the one to be praised for what happened to him. All the glory belongs to

God. It was God who saved our son, and it was God who decided to allow him to stay on this planet longer. People have told us over the years that God must've had big plans for Kennedy to have saved him and returned him to life. Amy and I have always said that whether Kennedy grew up to be the next Billy Graham or a ditchdigger who shared the gospel with the man in the ditch next to him, he would be following God's mighty plan.

We also want to be clear that none of Kennedy's story would have any significance apart from the truth found in the Bible. Without that, all we have here is just a nice story about a kid beating the odds. Taken apart from the Word, Kennedy's story could be dismissed as merely the wild imaginings of a young child's unconscious mind. And yet, everything he said pointed us straight back to God's truth revealed in His inspired Word.

Amy

The memory of begging God to save my boy and return him to me will stay with me forever. At times I have seen grieving parents and felt guilty and unworthy that our family is still whole while others are stricken with grief. For months, even years after the accident, I would be consumed with fear in thinking something was going to happen to one of my children. Many nights after Kennedy's accident, I would go to his room late at night, lay my head on his tiny chest, and listen to his heartbeat. I felt responsible that I had allowed my child to drown and fearful that something bad would happen again. I still envisioned my little boy under the water, struggling and calling for me to help him.

When fear and guilt would almost consume my body, I would rebuke Satan in the name of Jesus Christ, just as I had rebuked that evil spirit in Kennedy's hospital room. As I clung to the truths found in God's Word, I was able to break through the stronghold of condemnation, guilt, and unworthiness with confidence in knowing those things are not from the Lord. Satan tried to rob me of my joy with his lies, but the truth was firm ground under my feet.

Sometimes it grieves me to share Kennedy's story, because so many parents have lost their children, and I cannot explain why my child was saved when so many others were not. When my brother died, my own mother had to watch helplessly as cancer stole her son away from her. As much as I'd cried over losing my brother, I had no idea what it was like for my mom until I nearly lost Kennedy. Months after Kennedy's recovery, I called my mother, sobbing, and apologized to her: "Mama, I had no idea...the level of your pain." Before Kennedy's accident, I remember getting frustrated with my mother's grief at times—it was as though she forgot that she still had four other children and twelve grandchildren. Now I understood. So when we praise God for Kennedy's life, we always want to be so careful and respectful, knowing that others have lost a child and that we can only partially understand their pain.

> *Satan tried to rob me of my joy with his lies, but the truth was firm ground under my feet.*

We prayed for Mark to be healed every bit as fervently as we prayed for Kennedy's healing. Why the outcome was different, we will never know this side of heaven. But my prayer is that KeKe's story will comfort those who have lost a loved one, especially a child. Kennedy had no recollection of any pain or struggle during the drowning. His first memory after the accident was flying up to see Jesus. And when he saw his uncle Mark, he saw that he had been healed, just like we prayed for. Our prayer is that Kennedy's experience can serve as a reminder that God redeems all things and that those who have gone to be with the Lord are now happy and free from all suffering.

A Turtle in the Kitchen

Amy

One last thing.

When I was feeling so guilty and sad and angry at myself while Kennedy fought for his life, I kept going back to that moment when I'd scolded him about touching the baby with "turtle hands." Kennedy is in his twenties now, and he promises me he doesn't even remember my fussing at him, but oh, I do! Even though I know the blood of Jesus has already been poured out for my impatience in that moment, many times I have wished that I could take back those sharp words I spoke to my sweet KeKe, my precious gift from the Lord!

At the hospital, so many friends and family brought little gifts for Kennedy and for us. One lady brought me a stuffed animal—a cute little plush baby turtle. Of course, she had no idea that the "turtle hands" conversation had even happened and how it had pierced my heart. She just thought it was cute and hoped it would remind me that she loved and cared for me. And it would be a reminder, for the rest of my life.

When we got home from the hospital, I immediately put that turtle next to the coffeepot by our kitchen sink where I couldn't miss it. It's been there for over twenty years now, and when I look at it each morning, it reminds me to always carefully consider my tone of voice, especially with my beloved family. It reminds me how quickly we can speak careless words that we may spend a lifetime regretting.

Perhaps that stuffed turtle is just a small afterthought in a story as big as Kennedy's. But for me, the turtle in my kitchen will always have a special place in my heart—a reminder from God to treasure His blessings. How great is our God that He speaks to us in ways both great and small.

My Life since My Near-Death Experience

Kennedy Buettner

I was a little kid when I had my NDE. I remembered it up until I was about twelve or thirteen, but then I couldn't remember it anymore. I know the story like I know my own name, but I can't remember the actual experience.

Just because I can't remember the details doesn't mean it's not something I ever forget, though. I think about it especially whenever I go swimming or I'm near a pool.

Q *Do you remember your mom's reaction when you told her what you saw? That you met Jesus and your uncle Mark?*

A I don't remember her reaction, whether she was in shock or disbelief, but I do remember that she got a pen and paper and wrote down everything I said, word for word. Then one day, she gave me some paper and crayons, and I drew a picture of what I saw in heaven. She didn't tell me to draw it; I just wanted to.

Q *You and your parents have talked about your NDE over the years. Has living through it in an earthly life been challenging?*

A My parents and my family are very involved in our church. My parents told people about my experience and what I witnessed. People thought I was special because I went to heaven and saw Jesus. But for much of my life, I didn't want to be "special" and build myself up with pride. I had to struggle not to play the "locally famous" card with my friends because I was kind of like the local Harry Potter: the boy who lived. Sometimes it was hard not to give in to that. I tried to be humble, but I could sometimes feel myself struggling.

The other thing that was hard was growing up in the Bible Belt and in a Christian family and big church community, where I never had to defend myself from skeptics. When I went to New Zealand after college to do mission work (I was twenty-two at the time), I found myself in a very atheistic culture. I shared my near-death experience and some people challenged me on it. They weren't confrontational, but they also weren't totally open to accepting a story like this.

While I was there, I became friends with a New Zealander and told him I had a testimony to share with him. Afterward, he said, "That's cool for you, but I don't know if I believe that. It could've been a dream or just something that happened in your brain." It was the first time I'd ever gotten that reaction. For about half a second, I considered what he said, and then I thought, *No, a four-year-old wouldn't have known all that stuff.*

⁓

Q *Many adult experiencers reveal that they returned with a greater sense of love and peace. Do you remember how you felt when you left the heavenly realm and returned?*

A I don't recall the exact feelings I had when I woke up and remembered my NDE. I didn't have a real relationship with Jesus until I was a teenager, but I don't think that was a result of my near-death experience. When I got older and reflected on the experience, I did have that sense of peace and love toward God, knowing that my life is His and He has control of it. But that came when I was around eighteen or nineteen and really started to have a relationship with Jesus.

I didn't become a Christian until the summer after my freshman year in college. That was when I finally said, "This isn't just my parents' God; this is going to be my God." In the Bible Belt, most people grow up in church, but you have to grow up into your own faith. For me, the moment came when I was at the beach doing mission work with Campus Outreach. I was talking with the leader of the group, who knew me well and was a friend of mine, about my faith and how I was a Christian, because I thought I was. But he knew that I was living my life like the average college student instead of truly walking with the Lord. He said, "If you're a Christian, I would love to hear your testimony." So I told the story of my NDE from when I was four, and I waited for him to be impressed, like everybody always was.

In Hebrews 4:12, the Bible tells us that "the word of God is alive and active. Sharper than any double-edged sword, it penetrates even to dividing soul and spirit, joints and marrow." And this was my Hebrews 4:12 moment, when my heart was pierced so sharply, because my friend calmly said, "That's cool, but what has your faith been like from the age of five to now?"

And I said, "Oh, I've been on five mission trips, and I go to church and I always went to youth group when I was in middle school and high school." And then he told me, "That doesn't explain anything about your relationship with Jesus."

That's when it hit me. I had done the work, but I had never truly given myself over to God. To be honest, I'd signed up for the mission work because it was at the beach and there would be cute girls. But from that moment, everything changed.

⁓

Q *What is the most inspiring thing you remember about your NDE?*

A We read in the Bible and are told that there is life after death, that those who follow Jesus will go to heaven. And I saw what happens after death. I know that in heaven, people will be happy, and I know that is my future and the future for those who live in Jesus.

⁓

Q *Do you feel that God had a purpose for you since He gave you a glimpse of heaven and your beloved uncle Mark?*

A I remember that during my NDE, my uncle Mark or Jesus said, "It's not your time yet." Then Uncle Mark pushed my chest and I went back down the portal/whirlpool thing and passed through my mom's body. She was sitting on the couch next to my hospital bed. I remembered it vividly for many years, but I can't remember it now.

But that part of the story is so impactful for me. I feel like God must have sent me back so that I can share Jesus with people. I don't have to be perfect, but I do feel like I need to do my best to try to be worthy of being sent back here. But it's not like God told me, "Hey, go do this or that."

⁓

Q In thinking about your NDE, do you remember any aspects of it that at the time didn't make sense but now do? What were those?

A I told my mom about seeing the ladder and seeing angels. When I was twelve or thirteen, I came across the story in Genesis 28 about Jacob and the ladder, and I thought, *Oh, cool! I'm pretty sure I saw that!*

Little things I've learned about heaven in Bible class have reminded me of the things I saw. And later I found out that my uncle Mark's nickname had been "Buckmaster" because he was an avid hunter, and the doctor who was in charge of taking care of me at Children's Hospital was named Dr. Buckmaster, so that was an interesting piece to put together years later.

Also, when I was a little boy, I didn't understand that people were fully healed in heaven, but I saw my uncle fully healed, and now I know that scripture supports that.

Q Do you think your NDE affected your relationships?

A I think it probably changed things with my brothers, especially my oldest brother, Jacob. I feel like he was really protective of me, but there's really no way to know how he would've been if I hadn't drowned and had my NDE. All my siblings joke that I'm our parents' favorite because I died and came back to life! Of course, I don't actually think that, and if you ask Mom, she always says she "perfectly loves all of us completely," but my brothers and sister still joke about it. It's hard to say if I get my way more or not because I'm part of the majority party: with four brothers, my sister, Isabelle, is totally outnumbered!

Prayer Matters

By Yvonne Nachtigal, as told to Stephanie Thompson

Prayer delights God's ear; it melts His heart.

Thomas Watson

"Oh, Michael! My head!" I put my elbows on the table and cradled my head in my hands. My husband and I were at a fast food restaurant that evening when I felt an intense pain, as if a gigantic rubber band had snapped across my brain. I'd experienced recurring health challenges for the past five years, but lately these episodes of headaches, dizziness, and muscle weakness happened more frequently.

I'd gone to four different doctors and had two emergency room visits to try to diagnose this mysterious condition. One physician suspected midlife hormone fluctuations, but my blood test came back normal. I'd tried vitamin B-12 injections, swallowed routine doses of Excedrin daily, and exercised. I arranged to work from home in an attempt to reduce stress, took breaks from my computer screen, and ate cans of tuna for an extra protein boost. But no matter what I did, the fatigue and excruciating headaches persisted.

Desperate for answers, I talked to God. I'd had a strong faith since the time I was a child. I was a person who believed in the power of prayer. As the Bible says in Mark 11:24: "Therefore I tell you, whatever you ask in prayer, believe that you have received it, and it will be yours." I trusted that the Bible was true, but I sometimes wondered if God heard my prayers. I rarely saw evidence that He was listening, as many of my requests went unanswered. I wondered if prayer really made a difference, or if my prayers mattered at all. Throughout my fifty years, I'd traveled the gamut of doctrines on how prayer worked.

My childhood prayers were much like a Christmas wish list sent to a big Santa Claus in the sky, or *Der Weihnachtsmann,* as I called him thanks to my German upbringing. I metaphorically crossed my fingers and hoped that my requests would find favor with the Almighty. In church as a teen, I learned that confession of sin had something to do with whether a prayer

> *I wanted to do whatever I could to stay in God's good graces and receive His blessings.*

was granted or not. Then, as an adult, I heard about fasting for a breakthrough, that somehow missing meals could manipulate what the Lord did in a given situation. Preachers taught about inviting God's will as we surrendered our own. I didn't fully understand how suppressing my own desires and accepting another outcome could be attributed to the will of God.

To be honest, I couldn't make heads or tails out of how prayer worked. So I did it all—prayed daily, tried to keep "fessed up," occasionally fasted, and told God "His will, not mine," hoping to open the floodgates of heaven. I wanted to do whatever I could to stay in God's good graces and receive His blessings so He would answer my prayers.

Over the years, God had answered some of my smaller prayers, like when I prayed for a parking place and one appeared or when I asked for a job after weeks of looking and found one. But for the past five, I'd had a major request. God had remained silent. Not only had my prayers for good health gone unanswered, but my headaches worsened.

As I sat with Michael that crisp November evening in 2010, the knife-like jab on the right side of my head ballooned into a pulsating headache. My vision blurred. I felt nauseated.

Michael looked at me from across the hard plastic table and nodded. He tried to be supportive, but I saw doubt in his eyes. We'd had several conversations about the possibility of me being a hypochondriac. Since doctors couldn't find anything physically wrong, I, too, wondered if the pain in my head was *all in my head*. Could I somehow be exaggerating my symptoms or making it all up?

"You'll be better once we get home," he assured me. I took his elbow as we walked to our car.

The throbbing in my head was insufferable, but just as unbearable was that my reality was again being questioned, stirring unwanted memories. I'd grown up amidst difficult and confusing circumstances that I didn't fully understand.

Transcontinental Upbringing

I was born in Hamburg, Germany, the granddaughter of a Lutheran pastor who was part of the Confessing Church movement that protested Hitler and his *Reichskirche*, a unified state church espousing a doctrine compatible with Nazism to make churches an instrument of Nazi propaganda and politics.

Opa Teo, my grandfather, was arrested four times for speaking out against the Nazis. He died from his weakened health as a result of those imprisonments. My mother, only twelve at the time, and her three younger siblings were left traumatized. Starving and terrified, they hid from soldiers, gunfire, and bombs with their mother, my *Oma* Minchien, in war-torn Brachwitz, a village outside of Halle on the Saale River. The horror of the war, coupled with a harsh German upbringing, scarred my mother. Physically, she was a beautiful woman (often compared to the actress Donna Reed, who starred in *It's a Wonderful Life*), but she was emotionally damaged.

To escape the oppressive communism of East Germany, Mom defected when she was seventeen. While traveling with a choral group

> *Physically, my mother was a beautiful woman, but she was emotionally damaged.*

that had crossed the border to perform in the West, she snuck away to live with a relative in Hamburg. Soon after, she met and married my father. I came along shortly after. My parents divorced when I was an infant, so I never knew my birth father.

"*Yvilein, meine kleine knuddelpuppe, nur du und ich,*" she'd coo, as she tucked me in on the orange sofa bed that we shared in our one-room apartment. Yvi was my nickname, and adding "lein" to a name was a German term of endearment. "My little cuddle doll, it's just you and me," she'd remind me often. The two of us together, against the world.

In 1960, Mom met an American while he was visiting Europe. He was, as she understood, a traveling missionary. They married and moved to his hometown of Rexburg, Idaho, when I was five.

Mom's English was as poor as my new father's German, so there was a significant language barrier that resulted in Mom and me naively joining the Mormon Church, where Dad, his parents, grandparents, and generations of ancestors had all been members.

Life in the United States

Living in America was grand. I was thrilled to have a father. Dad showered me with loads of attention. He made me feel adored, like I was his special girl. A talented mechanic, his hobby was fashioning old cars into hot rods. He generously worked on engines for friends and women who couldn't afford the cost of a traditional garage. He was good with his hands and could fix or build anything, some things better than others.

That first winter, Dad made me a homemade sleigh—plywood sheets painted red with homemade skids crafted from welded metal rods. I treasured it. Even though it sank into the snow rather than gliding down the snow-covered bank in Rexburg Park, I didn't mind. The love he put into it shone through. I was proud that I mattered enough for him to build it just for me.

Shortly after our arrival in America, Dad arranged for me to have a much-needed eye operation. I was born with strabismus, severely crossed eyes. My right eye gazed at my nose instead of working in tandem with my left eye.

The procedure uncrossed my eyes, but even with eye exercises three times a day, I never gained depth perception. Still struggling with poor vision, I had to wear glasses. Today, I still rely on my dominant left eye to see. My right eye is much weaker and for all practical purposes is only useful for peripheral vision.

My brother was born that first year we arrived in the States. I adored being a big sister and doting on him. Once Mom understood the doctrinal differences she had with the Mormons (and hating the harsh winters in Idaho), she begged Dad to move. We eventually settled in Torrance, California.

> *Mom imparted in me a love for God.*

Mom loved being a homemaker. She baked delicious German pastries and encouraged me to invite friends over for a treat. I often picked flowers for her on the way home from school. I was so proud that she was my mother.

But as I grew up, she began to have increasingly critical, angry outbursts that I didn't understand. In contrast, my father was gregarious, outgoing, playful, and popular. Dad became my preferred parent.

In 1964 he joined the police force. His helpful and caring nature suited his occupation perfectly. Everyone loved him, including me.

To be fair, my dad did have a glaring passive-aggressive streak. He was over-the-top vindictive. "Don't get mad, get even" was his motto. If anyone wronged him, or if he perceived that someone slighted or judged him, he'd retaliate mightily. Not only would the offender get a ticket, but Dad made sure that everyone in their family would be ticketed for the mildest infraction. Since he was a policeman, he felt that he was above the law.

Although we didn't attend regular church service, because of my parents' differing views on religion, Mom imparted in me a love for God. I adored flipping through the pictures of Jesus in the German children's Bible that my oma gave me before we left Europe—pictures of Christ with little children sitting on His lap and the somber Good Friday crucifixion as He hung nailed to a cross. But my favorite was the scene with the brilliant light of heaven's holiness illuminating Christ at the resurrection. Gazing at the page, I could practically feel the intense love that radiated from that dazzling light. Somehow, I knew that heaven would be like that—filled with light and love.

The summer before I entered high school, Mom, my brother, and I joined Pacific View Baptist Church. I heard the Gospel at the youth Bible study in 1971 and eagerly trusted Jesus Christ for my salvation. A few months later, something evil started happening—something that would color my life and my relationship with my family forever.

Heartbreaking Abuse and Rejection

Starting in 1971, I endured years of abuse from my family. I was thirteen and no longer an innocent child. The atmosphere in our home became heavy. Mom's critical, angry outbursts were the norm now, her previous, nurturing side rarely surfacing anymore. Dad remained cheerful and upbeat, but took every opportunity to talk negatively about me when he thought I wasn't listening, to blame me when anything went wrong, or to discount my feelings when I tried to share about something that happened at school.

I didn't know how to process the dysfunction in my family. A myriad of emotions—confusion, shame, guilt, and betrayal—covered me. I felt abandoned, orphaned, alone. Rejection from both of my parents seared through me. Even my brother started to reject me. I was considered the black sheep.

For the rest of my life, any problems within the family, or my parents' marriage, were deemed my fault. I was branded as an outsider, the odd man out. The praises I used to receive from Dad were now heaped on my brother. My parents blatantly began to favor him over me.

> *I had a long-standing prayer that I recited every night:* God, get me out of here.

There was no one I could confide in, not even God. But I did have a long-standing prayer that I recited every night: *God, get me out of here.*

Leaving Home

Eager to escape my dysfunctional family environment, I searched for someone to fill the void. I daydreamed of having a family of my own with a husband who loved me and children who would be loved, their feelings fiercely protected.

Tom and I met at a party on Hermosa Beach. He was a struggling musician, a drummer in a rock band. I thought he was so cool with his flowing blond hair and quirky personality. All we had in common was a love of seventies rock music and unhappy home lives that made us both feel misunderstood. We got married and moved in together as soon as I graduated high school. I was a hostess at Bob's Big Boy; he worked at an electronics company during the day and played in a band on weekends.

Tom had no religious upbringing and even though I still believed in God, I became a casual Christian. Doing what I wanted to do, I shoved my faith to the side. I didn't think about going to church, reading my Bible, or praying much at all. I was young and in love, and life was going my way. I guess I didn't reach out to God because I didn't need anything. That changed after our son, Aaron, was born. My precious little babe was the apple of my eye. It was important to me to raise him in the church. We found Hope Chapel, a foursquare church in Hermosa Beach.

Tom liked the contemporary worship music, and I enjoyed the intimate prayer groups and the more charismatic fellowship. But some aspects of the church confused me. I didn't understand the "tongues" that many people prayed in. When other members claimed to have "a word from God" for me, I wondered why the Lord simply hadn't told me Himself.

When Aaron was two, we moved to Sacramento. I visited several denominations searching for true, biblical Christianity. I yearned to know God better and gain insight into how He answered the prayers of His people—people like me. Even though Tom went to church with us, he often complained that settling down with a family had deprived him of his dreamed-of music career. He ridiculed me by calling me "church lady" when I expected our family to attend weekly.

Four years after Aaron was born, our beautiful Brittany came along. The four of us saw my parents a few times when the kids were young, mostly on holidays, but they were cold when we visited and critical of how we were raising our children (with love, which they called "cod-dling," instead of the sarcastic tone that had marked their interactions with me). I was almost always the one who initiated calls. Some years went by without us even seeing them—not even an invitation to spend holidays together.

Why, God? became my frequent prayer as I learned about the lavish love and earthly possessions they heaped on my brother and his children, while shunning me and my family, who lived in humble circumstances. Their excuse was that we had moved away. But living near them had been unbearable, with their disapproval of me extending to my children.

Five years later, Tom and I started marriage counseling. I told the counselor about my strained relationship with my family, especially my father since he was the one I was closer to growing up, and how this was affecting my life. After several weeks I wrote a letter to my dad, at the urging of my counselor.

> *My reconciliation with my dad was the most freeing and wonderful thing. I was on top of the world!*

One night that same week, our doorbell rang at 10 p.m. Dad stood on the porch. He'd driven six hours to our house in the San Francisco Bay area

"I thought we could talk," he said.

I followed him out to his pickup so we could have privacy from my family, and we drove toward the Delta.

"So I read your letter..."

He kept his eyes on the road as he reflected back to me the situations and feelings I'd written. His lips quivered as he confessed to his bad behavior. We parked at the edge of the water.

"I only hope that one day you can forgive me, Yvonne."

Tears rolled down his cheeks. I saw how hard it was for him.

"Of course I forgive you! I love you, Dad!"

I hugged his neck as he sobbed. We headed back to my house, where Dad stayed the night on our couch.

He was so sincere. Our reconciliation was the most freeing and wonderful thing. I was on top of the world! *Praise You, Father! Thank You, Lord!* I was thrilled to have my dad back after all this time.

Tom and I drove down to my parents' house with the kids for the Easter holiday a couple of months later. Surprisingly, my parents still treated us coldly, like they didn't want us there. It was as if my father's apology had made no difference in our relationship—if anything, my mom and brother treated us even worse, as though I'd done something terribly wrong. I was befuddled.

Christmases, birthdays, special occasions passed again without invitations. I resigned myself to the fact that they just didn't want anything to do with me.

The culmination of my family's indifference and my marital difficulties left me feeling isolated and rejected. I became disillusioned with organized religion too. It seemed like the church's answer to my struggles was that it was all somehow my fault. *I should turn the other cheek to love and honor my parents despite the way they treated me. If I were a more godly wife, my marriage would change.*

In 1995, Dad died as a result of complications following heart surgery. He was only fifty-five.

I sank into a depression. Despite counseling, Tom and I divorced months later, after seventeen years of marriage. Having been taught that irreconcilable differences was not God's approved reason for the dissolution of a marriage, I was filled with guilt and shame. I didn't want to be single. I yearned for a husband with whom I could share my life. Looking at other happy families, I felt jilted. *It wasn't fair!* I'd been damaged by family and left incapable of wisely choosing a mate. I trusted that God would "work all things together for good" (as it says in the book of Romans) and heal me and my marriage. He had not. Didn't He hear my prayers? Was God listening at all?

After that, I quit going to church and stopped trying to live a life that the church and His Word had laid out for me. Sure, I believed God loved me, but it was clear that I was on my own.

Starting Over

The doctor had prescribed a high dose of antidepressants to carry me through the divorce and the death of my dad. In an effort to stabilize my mood, the medication clipped the emotional highs and lows of life that I once felt. My pervasive sadness was gone, but so was my conscience and happiness. I felt flat. It had been eighteen months on the medication and I still felt lost.

I wanted to get my life back, so I stopped taking antidepressants cold turkey, even though my doctor advised against it. A side effect of the sudden withdrawal from the medication is sleeplessness. I couldn't sleep for weeks.

One evening, during this period, I finished my shift at the pub where I was working. To wind down, I sat at the bar and sipped a pint of beer. Insomnia and alcohol were a bad mix. I had no business being on the streets. I should have known better, but I drove up to Silver Creek Falls. It was a mountainous road and I was driving too fast. I crossed an icy bridge and my car started to slide out of control. Showers of sparks flew all around me as the sides of my car raked against the metal guard rails.

The car began to spin. I turned the steering wheel in the direction of the skid. The car straightened out, but propelled me toward a huge pine tree. I pumped the brakes. They didn't respond due to the icy conditions. My body trembled with fear as I braced for impact, prepared to die. Just before I crashed into the tree, the car mysteriously jolted to a stop. The force threw me to the floorboard. (I wasn't wearing a seatbelt. Another bad choice.)

With the sun close to the horizon, I turned off the ignition and staggered out of the car, still shaking. Standing on the deserted roadway, I surveyed the situation. I couldn't imagine what had

> *Just before I crashed into the tree, the car mysteriously jolted to a stop.*

stopped my car from careening into the tree. There was nothing visible that could have made me stop so abruptly.

I walked around and looked at the tires. No blowouts, but the rubber tread had been worn away from all four tires and only the pure metal steel belts remained. I scrunched down and examined the undercarriage of the vehicle. Nothing was damaged. *Surely something caused such an abrupt stop?* But I found nothing. Amazingly, I had no injuries.

That night was a wake-up call. My out-of-control car had miraculously stopped eighteen inches before smashing into a huge pine tree. For no apparent reason. It was unexplainable. I had no idea how it happened, other than it had to have been God.

I knew then that I desperately needed to get my life together. I found another job, started going to church, made friends who shared a belief in God, and began to read my Bible. Months later, a mutual acquaintance wanted Michael and me to meet. I wasn't ready for a relationship, so we got to know each other through daily calls. His kids were grown and on their own, and he was a concert tour manager who traveled a lot and planned to move to Scotland in the coming weeks—another good reason to keep our friendship platonic.

We talked on the phone for a couple of weeks. We had never laid eyes on each other, but our personalities really clicked. I told him I wanted to get my life back on track and that I wasn't looking for romance. He was a Christ-follower on that same path of seeking to build his spiritual life.

He pushed to get together in person. The first two times he planned a date with me, I bailed. Instead of meeting him for dinner, I drove past the restaurant and came right back home. I did the same thing a week later when he arranged to meet for a movie. I just didn't have it in me to date and told him so.

Days later, he tried a third time. Michael invited me to a Kenny G concert.

"I'll pick you up," he said, now savvy to my reluctance.

This time I went. I had a fabulous time. We both loved music and had so much in common. With Brittany in high school and Aaron recently married and on his own, Michael and I married five months later.

Unexplained Health Issues

My headaches started in 2005, seven years into our marriage. Brittany was now grown and married, so Michael and I moved to Vista, California. I worked as a graphic designer for a Southern Baptist church. My "office" was a five-by-seven-foot utility closet that housed the computer server. The workspace was created with the best of intentions so I could shut the door and work undisturbed.

After a few months, I started having painful back spasms, headaches, and anxiety attacks. I chalked it up to spending too much time hunched over my keyboard. I'd often leave early to finish my work at home. I pushed my boss to allow me to work remotely, but even that didn't help—my symptoms persisted. I made an appointment with my family practitioner, but she had no answers. I even ended up in the emergency room a couple times because of unbearable migraines and projectile vomiting that accompanied them. The ER physician ordered a spinal tap to check for an aneurysm. The doctors couldn't find anything physically wrong with me.

I was desperate for an answer, but like so many other times in my life when I'd prayed, God was silent.

Although the medical personnel didn't say anything, I had the distinct impression they thought I was making it up—that my physical ailments were all in my mind. I cried out to God. "Father, please show me what's wrong." I was desperate for an answer, but like so many other times in my life when I'd prayed, God was silent.

After dealing with headaches and fatigue for four years, I noticed the ring finger on my left hand began to tremor. When I showed my family doctor, she acted concerned and said we should keep an eye on it. I'd also started experiencing spells of extreme weakness that debilitated me for days. It took an incredible effort just to shower and get dressed. The doctor ran blood tests and discovered that I had a vitamin deficiency. I hoped B12 shots would be the answer. But the headaches and weak spells continued. The tremor in my finger got worse.

I'd lived on the West Coast for most of my life, and Michael and I had been in the San Diego area for a decade, but the recession of 2008 hit hard. In April 2009, we packed our two dogs, four parakeets, and one canary into our small car and moved to the Nashville area for Michael's work, since many recording artists lived there.

The people in Tennessee were so friendly. I loved the Smoky Mountains and the lush green landscapes. Our neighbors were welcoming. In fact, the woman across the street invited me and my two dogs to join her in the evenings as she walked her dogs. It was exciting to start a brand-new chapter.

> *The people in Tennessee were so friendly. It was exciting to start a brand-new chapter.*

We joined Gateway Community Church in Goodlettsville. We became part of a fabulous group called Friends of God (FOG). There were about twenty-five of us who met weekly and spent an hour or more together studying the Bible and praying for each other.

We'd been in Tennessee for only twenty-two months when the crippling fatigue caused me to start missing church. I became housebound.

We had lost our health insurance, so I was referred to the Salvus Center, a faith-based primary care clinic where medical professionals charge patients based on a sliding scale of what they can afford. The doctor there ran more blood tests, but still couldn't find anything. I concluded that my symptoms must be psychosomatic. So did Michael, who thought I was a hypochondriac. I often broke down, crying in frustration and humiliation when my exhaustion and headaches were too much for me to handle. *Why can't I control something that's not real? Something that's all in my mind?*

One evening at our FOG home group, I sat in a chair in the middle of the circle. Everyone surrounded me, laying their hands on my head, shoulders, arms, and back. They prayed fervently for my health. For healing. This group became the extended family I'd craved. They were faithful friends and prayer warriors. Everything was so different here in Tennessee. Everything except my health problems.

A Mysterious Voice

In early December 2010, my symptoms got worse. I had gone into the kitchen for a yogurt. As I reached for the refrigerator handle, my left arm shot off to the left, a few feet beyond the fridge. I grasped the air. My heartbeat quickened. I couldn't control my own body. Quick tears formed in the corners of my eyes.

"Michael! Something's really wrong with me," I shouted. "It's like my arm has a mind of its own. I totally missed the fridge handle when I reached for it."

"I'm sure it's nothing," he answered, not getting up from the living room couch.

I stood still as a statue, frozen in the kitchen. Tears ran down my cheeks. I tried to stifle my sobs. I felt so afraid. So alone. So misunderstood.

"Soon it will be clear. Then it will be over."

A voice. God's voice. I felt suspended in time as the familiar voice of the Lord whispered firmly into my mind. Immediately my cries stopped. Feelings of peace rained down from heaven. *God knows what is happening to me.* Comfort like a warm blanket enveloped me. The source of my mysterious illness would soon be revealed! I might have questioned whether or not God heard my prayers, but I didn't doubt that the Lord had just spoken to me.

It was at that moment that I understood the truth. Something *was* indeed wrong with me. I wasn't lying. I wasn't a hypochondriac. I wasn't making it up. Whatever the outcome, God heard me. He saw my physical ailments. I was in His hands.

A Long-Awaited Diagnosis

My physical condition continued to deteriorate to the point that I couldn't balance without support. I'd almost lost complete control of my left hand. My left leg was weak and would buckle under me when I tried to stand.

Christmas was coming, but I had no energy to decorate, bake, or shop for my children or grandchildren, who were still on the West Coast. I was heartbroken that my life had been reduced to this. I had to do something. I was only fifty-three.

Lying in bed, I called the Salvus Center and booked an appointment for December 28.

Once there, I waited in the exam room and clutched a folded piece of paper. I'd written a list of the symptoms I'd experienced over the last five years. I worried that if I recited the litany verbally, the doctor would think I was a hypochondriac. I unfolded the paper and double-checked to make sure I hadn't forgotten anything.

The technician asked for the reason for my visit. I handed her the page. A few minutes later, a grandfatherly looking physician introduced himself. He sat in the chair next to me. "Did you see the list of my symptoms?" I asked nervously.

He nodded. I held out my hand to show the tremor. He listened patiently as I explained my other ailments.

"I suspect there's something going on in your brain," he said gently. "You need to get to the hospital for a CT scan right away. We don't have the equipment here."

I exhaled, not in worry, but relief. *He doesn't think I'm crazy! He believes me!*

The doctor wanted to call an ambulance to transport me. I insisted I drive myself since the hospital was only a few blocks away and we couldn't afford an ambulance. By this time, I was so weak from exerting energy for the appointment that two people had to help me back to my car.

> *I exhaled in relief. He doesn't think I'm crazy! He believes me!*

Even though the hospital was only around the corner and down the street, my mind was so impaired that I went six miles out of the way. I prayed all the while, not sure I could make it.

When I finally found the emergency department, I leaned against the outside of the building as I walked. A nurse ran toward me with a wheelchair and took me inside.

After a CT scan of my brain, a doctor gave me the results.

He cleared his throat. "There's a mass in your brain—about four and a half centimeters in diameter," he said slowly, as if he struggled with the words.

"How big is that?" I asked.

He gestured with his thumb and forefinger. It looked to be about the size of a large egg. The doctor insisted on an ambulance to transport me to Skyline Medical Center, a neurological surgical hospital in Nashville, about forty minutes away.

I called Michael to let him know what was happening. He met me at our local hospital just before I got into the ambulance. With a furrowed brow and pale skin, he looked sicker than me. I worried he might pass out.

"Oh, Yvonne!" he cried, gripping my hand.

An incredible peace overshadowed my fear. I finally had an answer to why I'd been so sick. There was indeed something very wrong with me. Whatever the outcome, I knew God had heard me and was going to heal me. I clung to His promise in the kitchen: *Soon it will be clear and then it will be over.*

Post-Holiday Operation

At Skyline, I felt embarrassed to tell the admitting clerk we didn't have health insurance. I fully expected to be turned away. She smiled kindly. "We'll worry about that later. Let's just get you in a room." As a nurse wired me to monitors on the seventh floor, the room seemed to strobe. Bright, lightning bolt–like explosions danced across my field of vision. They were everywhere I looked.

"I'm seeing flashes of light," I said, my voice rising in alarm.

She turned off the television and flipped the light switch. The strobe instantly faded in the darkened room. As the IV fed steroids into my body to reduce the swelling around the mass, pain medication relieved the headache and body pain that had been my constant companions for the past six weeks.

I had a full-body CT scan and full-body MRI to look for more tumors or cancer. Michael stayed by my bedside, overtalking to cover his nervousness. He called my mom and my kids, as well as friends at our home group to let them know I had a brain tumor. Michael seemed terrified, but I had no fear. The peaceful feeling from the kitchen continued to envelop me.

The next morning a neurosurgeon, Dr. Spooner, walked into the hospital room. His tall frame filled the doorway.

"I'm glad to report that the scans show no other masses," he announced, pushing up his glasses. "But the mass is located deep inside your brain, close to the brain stem."

He stopped for a moment to let the information sink in.

Michael seemed terrified, but I had no fear. The peaceful feeling from the kitchen continued to envelop me.

"We need to remove it immediately," he said, carefully measuring his words. "We'll keep you on steroids for a few more days to get the swelling down before proceeding with the operation."

"Is it cancer?" I asked directly. After dealing with pain for so long, I didn't want him to sugarcoat the situation for my benefit.

Dr. Spooner smiled. His dark eyes radiated sympathy. "Because of its large size, the mass is most likely benign, but I can't be sure until we get it out. It has to come out."

I tried to lighten the heavy atmosphere by asking a silly question. "Will it hurt?"

"I can promise you a good headache!" He smiled as he quipped back.

The operation was scheduled the Monday after the New Year holiday, on January 3, 2011, six days later.

As I lay in the hospital bed, friends from our home group stopped by to encourage me. They relieved Michael daily. Even though it was the holiday week, between Christmas and the New Year, and our city was blanketed by sleet and snow, friends visited after work and after church services. They told me I was on prayer chains—that people were praying around the clock.

Fighting Fear

That Monday morning, January 3, 2011, a nurse awakened me for surgery at 4:30 a.m. The reality of the procedure sank in: a doctor was literally going to saw through my skull and dig out this mass from deep inside my brain.

The peace I'd felt during the last six weeks suddenly evaporated. Terror gripped me. My thoughts raced. *What if I never wake up? What if something goes wrong and I'm unable to see, speak, or hear after the operation? What if this surgery leaves me paralyzed? What if it changes my mental or emotional capabilities?* I choked back the sobs that erupted from deep inside my soul.

> *I felt like I was safe in the arms of God. Whatever my future held, I trusted God would hold me.*

"Lord Jesus," I prayed over and over. I couldn't find the words, but I knew God saw my fear. I started to recite every scripture that came to my mind: praise scriptures, promise scriptures, Jesus's words. I sang praise songs, and then I prayed for every single person I loved—my children, Michael and his children, Mom, my brother and his wife, our extended families, past friends, current friends, the hospital staff—everyone who came to mind. Nurses fluttered in and out—checking my blood pressure, monitoring my vital signs. They quietly smiled to reassure me. Within an hour, the peace that had carried me through the past six weeks returned. I felt like I was safe in the arms of God. Whatever my future held, I trusted God would hold me.

A hospital attendant came for me fifteen minutes before surgery. I glanced at the window and noticed the dark, overcast sky had begun to lighten with the approaching dawn. He rolled the gurney to the elevator that took us to the surgical floor. Michael waved to me from the hallway.

In pre-op, a nurse put my glasses on a bedside table as the anesthesiologist and surgical staff chatted away. The curtain was pulled back. Dr. Spooner joined the surgical team. The gurney rolled down the hall to the operating room. As the medicine in the IV hit my bloodstream, I relaxed. Voices faded to echoes, and I couldn't follow the conversation between the nurses and doctors. I entered the operating room with its bright lights flat on my back. The clank of medical equipment reverberated. Everything faded as the anesthesia pulled me into darkness.

On a Wing and Their Prayers

Suddenly, I was wide awake. I wasn't in the hospital. I was somewhere that was completely foreign and unworldly, yet at the same time, it seemed extraordinarily familiar. Like home. Awareness swept over me. I realized this was the place where I'd always belonged. I'd come home.

It took me a bit to get my bearings and realize I was in a different realm. I knew I was no longer in my body, no longer on earth. I also knew I wasn't dreaming. Unlike dream scenes that fade in and out and seem nonsensical or confusing, this experience was well organized, focused. I was acutely alert, more conscious than I'd ever been before. My thoughts were lucid.

Time seemed different in this place. My thoughts were sped up, incredibly fast. Everything happened at once. There was no before, during, or after. I instinctively knew that I was outside of the concept of time.

I sensed there was more for me to comprehend, but for the moment, I knew that life on earth had been a brief, created event. While important, it was not my true existence compared to this eternal one.

My senses were incredibly more vivid here. I felt the presence of God.

Unspeakable beauty surrounded me. A radiant light, brighter than the sun, shone all around me. The intensity should have been blinding, but it didn't hurt my eyes. My vision was different here too. In fact, my eyesight was keen despite the absence of my glasses. I could see things far in the distance and was able to examine things in close proximity on a microscopic level. As if I was looking through a brand-new magnifying glass, these tiny details stood out with perfect clarity—a far stretch from the poor vision that had plagued me all of my life. My senses were incredibly more vivid here. I felt the presence of God.

I was sitting up with my legs stretched out in front of me. *That's odd. Shouldn't I be lying on a hospital table?* I slowly came to realize that I was seated on an enormous wing, maybe sixty feet long, maybe bigger, but it didn't look anything like the wing of a bird. Intuitively, I knew the wing belonged to an angel. My angel. But the angel wasn't just a spirit. It had substance, made out of something that didn't exist on earth. I was fascinated by it.

Instead of being white and billowy, the wing was strong and impenetrable. Beautiful beyond description, it was one solid creation fashioned in the colors of autumn—bright and colorful hues: red, orange, gold, brown, and auburn. The colors were so vivid that they emanated light. I had never seen anything that equaled its beauty. Somehow, I knew there was nothing like this on earth.

The color palate surprised me. I would have expected shades of white and golden yellow or pastels of blues and purples like paintings I'd seen depicting the celestial realm. Perhaps those artists had never seen the heaven I saw or perhaps this wasn't heaven at all.

The wing reminded me of liquid gold, but it was hard and semi-transparent and glowed like embers, similar to an effervescent gemstone that emitted a fiery light. Deep coral veins, not like veins in a body but more like the veining in a slab of marble, ran through the wing. It was the most gorgeous thing I'd ever seen.

With childlike innocence and curiosity, I reached out my hand to stroke it. I wanted to feel its surface to further understand what this wing was made of. When I extended my arm and reached down my hand, though, I couldn't feel it at all. In fact, I didn't see my hand, despite having the impulse that I wanted to use my hand to touch the wing.

At that moment, I realized I no longer had a body. The thought crossed my mind: *I didn't make it.* But I wasn't upset or afraid. I was glad to be in this celestial sphere.

An overwhelming feeling of love engulfed me. It was a love like I'd never known before, but I somehow knew it always existed. I recognized it as the unconditional love of God. This incredible love surrounded me—strong and tangible, as if it were an actual substance. It was similar to the pure, unadulterated love I felt when I held my children as newborns, only the love here was more intense. This was the perfect love that God had intended for the world, but that sin had soiled and tainted. This was the love of which the Bible speaks—the love for which Jesus laid down His life.

This unstoppable love was directed toward me. It was all around me. Soothing, comforting, irresistible, it was all-powerful and intense.

Here I was able to see the love that I'd only been able to feel in the physical world, as if I were visibly experiencing it through the insight of my being, not with my eyes. My "seeing" in this place was similar to having a "knowing" on earth, like unexplained insight or knowledge.

The angel whose wing I sat on radiated with this great love too. It was everywhere. The entire atmosphere was filled with it. I somehow knew that this love was the natural and right state of things. It was life itself. There was no fear or sadness. The love brought me an indescribable rest and peace.

I realized that this wing and the angel it belonged to were what had held me through the pain of the past six weeks. Not "held" in the earthly sense, but a spiritual sort of being held, of being protected, guided. This angel had surrounded me from the time I heard God's voice in the kitchen to when the doctor announced there was a large mass in my brain. I realized then, too, that it had been with me throughout my life, only I hadn't been able to recognize it.

I looked around. I couldn't see the rest of the angel and thought that I maybe wasn't allowed to view more than its enormous wing and the dazzling, unearthly light. An awareness washed over me that the angel and everything else here was made out of light. Light was a substance.

Light was a life force. Jesus's words came to mind: "I am the light of the world."

Then I noticed an immense brown spot near the tip of its wing. I was puzzled by it. I had a sense that it was a wound and that the injury had something to do with me. *Did the spot occur when the angel was protecting me?*

Past the wing, I now saw farther. Beyond the radiant light was silence, pure blackness. Not anything specific in itself, just a lack of light, a deep blue-blackness, a void. Perhaps my mind could only take in this immense wing, filling my vision as far as I could see, the only visible light in the midst of the darkness. Even the emptiness, I sensed, held another place beyond this glorious light from where all the love emanated.

I knew there was a definite source of love. I had the knowledge that this source of love was God, even though I couldn't see Him.

As I became more oriented to my surroundings, I noticed there seemed to be a source, a point from which the love flowed. It was above me, over my shoulder on the right. Peace, joy, and comfort originated from a place on my lower left, as though these feelings were the outgrowth of the love. I didn't understand the significance of the directions, or separations of where these emotions emanated. I didn't know if they were related to the being that held me or something else, but I knew there was a definite source of love. I had the knowledge that this source of love was God, even though I couldn't see Him.

An immense realization overtook me as I recalled my life. Here in this place, it was as if everything that I'd done wrong never happened. I hadn't realized how heavily the memories of my sins and shortcomings had weighed on me. It wasn't that God ignored my sin. I truly understood at that moment what it meant that He exchanged it, abolished it with Jesus's sacrifice on the cross. And because of that, my sin was washed away. Obliterated. Totally forgotten, as if it never occurred.

Here, I was fully accepted and finally known. The only approval and love that mattered was from God. He accepted and loved me completely. For the first time in my life, I felt dearly loved with no strings attached.

Outside the magnificent glow of the angel, I peered into the nothingness. Still, I sensed there was more beyond this place. A faint sound, like a rushing of air or water gurgled off in the distance. My thoughts went back to the world from which I had come. I thought of my husband, my children, and the friends I'd left behind. I knew they would be heartbroken when news reached them that I had died, but I didn't

I knew they would be heartbroken when news reached them that I had died, but I didn't feel upset or worried for them.

feel upset or worried for them. Intuitively, I understood that God had them all in His care. They would be all right. My confidence in that knowledge was so strong that I considered them only briefly.

A series of brief tingling, like electrical sensations, quivered in the lower part of my left leg, making me aware that I was still in both worlds. I intuitively understood that I was sitting up on the operating table. I could see the surgeon standing behind me accessing my brain through the back of my head. *They're still working on me!* I had a fleeting thought that whatever the surgeon was doing affected the nerve in my leg.

The sensation caused me to look downward. As I looked in the direction of the tingling in my leg, I saw a crowd of people. They didn't look the way people did in the natural world. I knew they weren't the doctors and nurses in the surgical suite. They were similar to silhouettes, but three dimensional and made of thousands of small particles—not like the angel's wing, which was all one piece. I intuitively knew they were human. Each shadowy figure had some light mixed in, giving off a bit of the radiance that surrounded the wing in this place. I somehow understood these beings had a stake in both worlds.

I saw no details in the faces of these people, but as they moved and turned to the side, I saw noses, chins, various shapes and lengths of hair. I watched them move around and make gestures. Their mouths moved as they talked to each other, yet I couldn't hear or make out what they said. Somehow, I knew that they were people who were concerned about me. My heart filled with love for them.

While I looked at them, the angel spoke in a powerful yet gentle masculine tone. The voice sounded familiar, as if I'd known it all my life.

"The multitude is petitioning for you."

The words surprised me. They came out of nowhere. I didn't hear with my ears. Pure and righteous, the words were spoken into my being.

Even though I couldn't see anything more, I knew it was the angel who spoke the words. The silhouettes were people praying for me. They petitioned God on my behalf. They wanted me to come through the surgery and live.

But I wasn't sure that I wanted to return to my life. I could be content forever in this moment, in this love, joy, beauty, and glory, safely held on the angel's wing.

I looked downward, surveying the people again. I felt overwhelmed by their devotion and was filled with love and awe for so many who prayed for me. As I basked in that love, the angel spoke again.

This time, the voice sounded different—not as though the angel were giving information. This time, the angel spoke with authority, as if making an announcement.

"The petition is granted!"

Nervously Waiting—Michael's Perspective

I'd marveled at how calm Yvonne had been that week as she lay in a hospital bed at Skyline Medical Center and awaited brain surgery. *Brain surgery!* I could hardly believe it.

Guilt consumed me when I thought about the five years I didn't take her symptoms seriously. If I just would have been open to the possibility that something major was wrong with her, then maybe doctors would have caught the mass earlier and the situation would be less grave. When I met her last week in the emergency department, I was frozen with fear. Shocked at the news.

I grew up a country boy. Toughing it out was the way we coped. "Just cowboy up" was a popular saying in my youth. But there was no toughing it out this time. Yvonne had a massive tumor in her brain, after all. The slightest mistake by the neurosurgeon could mean a permanent loss of mental or physical functions. She could end up paralyzed or, worse, dead.

We didn't know if the mass was malignant or benign, either. If it was cancerous, she'd have to endure radiation therapy and maybe chemotherapy, in addition to recovering from the intricate surgery to remove the tumor from her brain. Dr. Spooner said recovering from this operation alone could take a year.

Besides the emotional toll of this surgery, a long, difficult recovery, and the possibility of complications or death, I also didn't know how on earth we would be able to pay for these medical services—a long hospital stay and a surgical staff that included two neurosurgeons, a plastic surgeon, and an anesthesiologist, along with nurses and technicians. No one at the hospital was mentioning costs, but I knew it would add up to hundreds of thousands of dollars. And we just didn't

I'm used to being the go-to guy, the man with the answers. But in this dire situation, I felt lost and powerless.

have that kind of money. It would take us decades to pay off the debt. Still, the mounting medical bills were easier to stomach than thinking about the possibility of losing my beloved wife.

I'm usually the calm one in our marriage. I'd been a concert tour manager for forty years. I know how to deal with a crisis. When we're on the road, I'm the one people come to when there's a problem. I'm used to being the go-to guy, the man with the answers. But in this dire situation, I felt lost and powerless.

Yvonne repeatedly said she had peace about the surgery—that whatever the outcome, God was in charge. I tried to stay positive. I kept my emotions in check when we were together, but when I went home in the evenings, I'd break down. I had no appetite, I had trouble sleeping, and I couldn't stop my mind from thinking about the what-ifs. The possibilities of what could go wrong in the operating room mocked me.

It was hard to concentrate and harder still to pray. I felt so blind-sided. *Why hadn't God led me to take her symptoms seriously? Why didn't He show me that she was really this sick? Couldn't He have somehow intervened to help her when she was seeking treatment years ago?*

The thought of losing her filled me with anxiety. *What if she doesn't make it?* I pushed down my fear. I knew all too well what it was like to have someone close to me, someone I loved, pass away.

My mom was thirty-nine when she died of an aneurysm. The blood clot started in her leg and hit her heart before anyone knew it. I'll never forget that horrible evening. Mom fell to the floor in the living room. Dad screamed for me and we lifted her onto the couch. I bolted up the street to get a neighbor who was a doctor. He followed me home, pounded Mom's chest, and tried to revive her using CPR. Near the end, Mom sat up straight. She threw her hands in the air and smiled wide, laughing. We all breathed a sigh of relief that she was still with us.

I was overwhelmed with gratitude that the doctor was able to revive her. Seconds later, she fell back on the couch. Mom was totally still. The doctor checked her pulse. She was gone.

Her death was a huge shock to our family. My mother was a committed Christian. She lived every moment to the fullest. I can't remember a time when she wasn't happy, regardless of our circumstances. I was just fifteen years old. Dad was beside himself, overwhelmed with grief. As the oldest, I had to be the responsible one and look after my two younger brothers and my little sister, who was only five.

The aneurysm took Mom so fast. There was nothing more that the doctor, my father, or I could have done. But it had been different with Yvonne. She had been sick for years and I never took her seriously.

When she called from the hospital and said they found a mass in her brain, it knocked me off my feet. I'd been a fool. I had no idea it was so severe. Guilt nagged at me. I should have listened to her. She'd suffered from debilitating headaches. What if I had made her get a CT scan years ago? The mass would have been smaller then. The surgery could have been easier. It was

"God, I can't bear to live without her. Please don't let her die."

hard not knowing how it all would turn out. Not knowing if Yvonne would be okay.

Mike Peasall, our pastor at Gateway Community Church, was a comfort to us both. He visited at the hospital and called me a couple times to check on Yvonne. He told me he was praying for us. In fact, the two-hundred-person congregation had formed a prayer chain—people petitioning heaven around the clock for the skill of the surgeon and the success of the operation.

Pastor was "believing for a full recovery" for Yvonne. It's a good thing we had him praying, and all those other people too, because I couldn't pray anything more than, "God, I can't bear to live without her. Please, don't let her die."

The night before Yvonne's surgery, I slept fitfully. I needed to get to the hospital about 6 a.m., but instead I awoke in a panic a little after 4 a.m., worrying about the surgery. Worrying about Yvonne.

What if she doesn't make it? Gripped with fear, I couldn't fall back to sleep. All I could do was lie there and worry.

Pastor Mike met me at the hospital that morning. So did Jerry Bryant, a nationally syndicated Christian radio show host. I hadn't talked to Jerry in a couple months and had no idea how he knew about Yvonne's surgery that morning.

A peppy nurse led us into a small surgery waiting area with about eight chairs. She sat at a desk and computer monitor. "I'll watch the surgery and be able to give you updates during the six- to eight-hour procedure."

I nodded and sank into a chair about five feet from her desk.

"They're getting ready to start," she said in a bubbly tone about twenty minutes later.

Pastor prayed with Jerry and me. "Lord God, guide the surgeon's hands. Protect Yvonne and let no harm come to her. We praise You for a successful operation. We give You the glory."

I couldn't focus on his words. I was too nervous to listen. Instead, my own prayer sprinted through my mind on an endless loop: *Please, God, don't let her die.*

> *I kept my eyes closed, praying that my intercession could somehow make a difference in the outcome.*

After about twenty minutes the nurse turned to me with the first update.

"Looks like it's going well." She put a finger on the earpiece that connected her to the audio in the operating room. She smiled and nodded enthusiastically at me.

I sighed and leaned back in the chair. I kept my eyes closed, praying that my intercession could somehow make a difference in the outcome of Yvonne's surgery. That God would hear my prayer and she'd be whole again.

About every fifteen to twenty minutes thereafter, the nurse turned to me and said something reassuring about what was happening in the operating room. Pastor Mike had another appointment, but said he'd check back later in the day. Praise God for Jerry! I can't imagine sitting there and waiting alone.

More than four hours had passed. I realized I hadn't had an update for a while. I looked over at the nurse. Her lips were pursed and her eyes stared solemnly at the monitor's screen. I checked my watch. She'd been silent for at least thirty minutes, maybe longer.

"Everything going okay in there?" I asked, hoping for a good word.

She put her hand on the edge of the monitor and turned it ever so slightly from my view.

"I...I'm sorry," she stammered, her optimistic tone now serious. "I don't have any updates right now."

What had gone wrong? Was Yvonne in danger?

Jerry and I exchanged looks. He bowed his head, and I watched his lips move silently. I turned and focused my eyes on the nurse, as if my gaze would resolve whatever issue was happening in the operating room. I couldn't bear to lose someone I loved again.

Ten to fifteen minutes later, the nurse's shoulders relaxed. She turned to me and smiled softly. "Looks like we're doing good," she said. "Things are going smoothly. They'll be finished quicker than expected."

A little over five hours after the start of the surgery, Dr. Spooner walked into the waiting area. He extended his right hand to me and grinned broadly. "I got it. Yvonne's waking up in post-op."

Thank You, God! For the first time in a week, I felt at peace.

My Awakening

My eyes popped open, but I quickly squeezed them shut again. I felt my body on the gurney, beneath a blanket. Women's voices chattered nearby. I realized I was in the recovery area, back at the hospital. *What happened?*

No longer was I in the celestial realm on an angel's wing. The brilliant light and splendid colors were now a mere memory, but the feelings of overwhelming love, peace, and joy lingered.

As the fog of the anesthesia lifted, I squeezed back tears. I felt conflicted. I wanted to be on earth with my family and my friends, while at the same time I longed to be back in that beautiful place. But the choice wasn't given to me. My fate had been decided—decided by the multitude who prayed for my life and by God, who granted their petition and sent me back to this world.

> *I'd experienced something remarkable, so life changing, that it would be impossible for me to keep quiet.*

"I was in heaven! I was in heaven!" I called from my post-op bed to anyone who would listen.

A nearby nurse whispered to her coworker. "She's saying she was in heaven."

Moments later, a woman in blue scrubs and a bouffant hair cap was by my side. She cupped my hand in hers and leaned near to my face.

"Sweetie, you're at Skyline Medical Center in Nashville, Tennessee," she said in an exaggerated tone. "We're not lettin' you go to heaven today."

Of course she didn't believe me, but for the first time in my life it didn't matter. Beyond a doubt, I knew the truth. I wasn't hallucinating. I wasn't making it up. I'd experienced something remarkable, so life changing, that it would be impossible for me to keep quiet. I had a bold confidence about what had happened to me, whether people believed me or not. I knew for certain I'd glimpsed glory.

Painful Recovery

As I further regained consciousness, I tried to move my legs and arms to see if I'd suffered any nerve damage. Everything seemed to be working.

I was transferred to the intensive care unit (ICU), where I sat up for a few hours so that my head could drain, according to Marshall, my nurse. All I could think about was what I'd seen and experienced in that celestial domain. I still felt like I was more in that realm than in this one.

"Can I get you anything?" Marshall asked before leaving my room.

"I wish I could hear praise music," I answered softly.

I longed for anything that might bring me back into that other reality, into God's presence.

"You're in luck," he said with a nod. "I've got you covered!"

He slipped out of the room. Moments later, he returned with a broad smile and his iPod. He helped me put in the earbuds. I pushed play.

Marshall's worship playlist rang out inside my head. Tears of joy streamed down my face. The prayerful tunes lifted my soul and spirit high above the pain and trauma. I traveled in my memory to the brilliant place where I sat safe and secure on the wing of my angel—the realm where I sat in the presence of God.

As I listened to the words of praise, healing poured over my body and my traumatized brain. Of course, I couldn't prove that the music clinically helped me, but I certainly felt better listening to it.

Marshall asked about my pain level. I gave him the thumbs-up signal. Still under the effect of anesthesia, and probably narcotics, my pain was minimal. But that wouldn't last long. My headaches before surgery were excruciating, but those were nothing compared to the pain I'd soon experience now that the procedure was over, according to Dr. Spooner.

Later that day, I was back in my room on the seventh floor.

"How are you feeling?" Dr. Spooner asked, as he walked to my bed-side to examine my incision. I had a massive cut from the top of my crown to the bottom of my neck.

In order to get to my tumor during the procedure, Dr. Spooner cut through the muscles on the back of my head and neck. He explained how a hole about the size of a silver dollar was drilled at the base of my skull. Through it, he slowly and meticulously used surgical tools to extricate the tumor that was lodged deep within my brain.

"Can I see it?"

Insatiably curious, I wanted to see the mass that had given me so much pain, and at the same time, allowed me to get a glimpse of the world beyond our own.

Dr. Spooner said that the tumor was removed pieces at a time, through a long tube because it was deep inside my brain, so there wasn't much to see. I was disappointed. He asked me to move my hands and feet, to smile and lift my eyebrows. He smiled, clearly pleased at the outcome of my surgery.

Still keeping his optimistic demeanor, he became a bit more seri-ous and looked into my eyes as he shared one small, yet concerning detail.

"A tiny part of the tumor was wrapped around a major artery. During the procedure, we started to have some trouble in that area. We made the decision to back out, so we had to leave a small portion of the tumor behind." He gestured with his thumb and forefinger to show a dimension roughly the size of a lima bean.

As I listened to his words, I recalled the sensation I'd felt in my left leg during my incredible visit to the other side.

"What do you mean, trouble?"

Dr. Spooner shifted his eyes to avoid my question. "Part of the tumor is still inside your brain. We'll continue to monitor it to make sure it doesn't grow."

"I bet that happened when I was in heaven," I said, ignoring his statement. "I was being held on the angel's wing and I felt something happening in my body."

> "I bet that happened when I was in heaven," I said. "I was being held on the angel's wing."

Dr. Spooner stood up straight and nodded. The look in his eyes made me think he attributed my experience to something other than a celestial visit.

"Those anesthesia drugs are pretty powerful. I'll check in with you tomorrow. I think you may be able to go home then," he said as he patted my arm.

After he left, I leaned back best I could given the bandage around my head and gazed out the window. The January trees were bare, but the natural world looked different to me now, a stark contrast to the spiritual world. My vision in the other realm had been perfect to the tiniest detail, so unlike my poor vision on earth. There, everything was made of light. But this world was fuzzy and dark—not crisp and sharp— even while wearing my glasses. Compared to the glory I'd glimpsed, it was as if someone had unplugged a Lite-Brite. I felt a deep sadness over the broken creation and how only a remnant of its splendor remained.

Yvonne's Miraculous Journey—
Michael's Perspective

An hour and a half after Yvonne's surgery was over, I was allowed to see her briefly in ICU. My wife looked small and frail sitting propped up in the bed surrounded by machines and monitors. A tangle of wires was attached to her body, as were IV lines administering pain medication and heart monitor wires poking out from her gown. She was groggy but in very good spirits—happy, even, with a huge smile on her face. I attributed her mood to the lingering anesthesia and potent narcotic painkillers.

She kicked her feet beneath the sheet and flapped her hands in the air.

> *An unexpected aura of peace rested in the room.*

"*Alles scheint zu funktionieren.*"

Yvonne's first language was German. I had no idea what she was saying.

"Honey," I whispered, as I walked close to the bed. "Say it in English."

"Everything seems to be working," she said, still waving her hands.

I laughed and kissed her cheek. Yvonne's mood put me at ease, but there was something else that felt calming to me. An unexpected aura of peace rested in the room. Despite being in the most serious wing of the hospital and just having had life-threatening surgery, Yvonne seemed to be clothed in tranquility and serenity.

Since ICU rules prohibited me from staying more than a few minutes, the nurse wrote my phone number on the whiteboard and sent me home. They promised to call if there were any changes in Yvonne's status overnight.

I tried to relax at home, but two concerns weighed heavily on me. First was Yvonne's health and continued recovery. Yes, she could come out of this totally healed, but the slightest mishap during surgery could cause her to become mentally impaired or emotionally damaged. *Lord, what if she doesn't make a full recovery?*

The second was finances. I had no idea what the total cost would be, but I knew there was no way we could afford the doctors, hospital, surgery, medication, and health-care bills that were starting to pile up. We'd lost everything in California when the economy tanked in 2008. We sold our half-a-million-dollar home for a fraction of what it was worth to move to Tennessee, where I hoped to find more work and the cost of living was reduced. Yvonne and I were self-employed. We rented our home and shared one car. We didn't even have health insurance, as we couldn't afford the premiums.

The next morning, Yvonne was in a regular room. I sat by her bedside. A hospital administrator stopped by. He held out his hand and introduced himself.

"Do you have a moment?" He motioned toward the doorway.

I followed him to the hall. He was wearing a sport jacket and had a rather rotund midsection and a beard. With his cheery demeanor, he reminded me of Santa Claus. We stood in the quiet corridor days after the New Year.

"Brain surgery to remove your wife's life-threatening tumor was a serious procedure," he said nodding. "Thankfully, Dr. Spooner is a renowned neurosurgeon. He had one of the most experienced surgical teams in the country assisting him."

I listened to his words, but had no idea where the conversation was going.

The man held out a page of paper.

I took it and scanned the numbers. It was Yvonne's bill. The charges totaled several hundred thousand dollars so far, and that was without all the surgery and physician costs. Beads of perspiration formed on my forehead. Yvonne would need follow-up appointments and tests once she was released. The costs would continue to climb.

> *The charges totaled several hundred thousand dollars so far, and that was without all the surgery and physician costs.*

"I explained to the admitting clerk that we didn't have insurance," I said, trying to keep my voice from shaking. I gave the administrator the details about our financial situation, including what happened with our house in California and how we were still struggling financially here.

"I see," he said. "Total costs won't be calculated until she's discharged, but they will be astronomical."

By this time my head was spinning, I felt the color drain from my face. I needed to sit down, but the hospital official didn't seem aware of my reaction.

"The good news is that here at Skyline we have a benevolence fund." He held out a stack of papers. "You can apply for assistance with paying the bill."

Even though he thought the total cost of treatment could end up being close to a half a million dollars, he felt like we would qualify to have a large portion of the costs covered by the fund.

I took the papers, breathed a sigh of relief, and went back into Yvonne's room. I was determined to fill out the paperwork quickly and turn it in with the proper documentation. For the first time in two years, I wasn't bitter about having lost so much on the sale of our home in California. A strange realization washed over me: had we held on to the house and waited for an offer to sell it at what it was worth, we wouldn't have qualified for the benevolence fund.

> *Thank You, God, for the blessing that didn't seem like a blessing at the time.*

As I sank into the recliner beside Yvonne (who was still sleeping), I chuckled at the irony. *Thank You, God, for the blessing that didn't seem like a blessing at the time.* I hoped the hospital administrator didn't just look like "the jolly old elf" but that he would be a metaphorical Santa who would deliver the biggest gift of our lifetime—my wife's health restored without a mountain of debt.

While Yvonne dozed, I made my usual daily call updates to family and friends who were praying. Unfortunately, Yvonne's mother hadn't been too supportive through her daughter's ordeal.

"Stop calling me with these melodramatic messages," she'd replied, when I phoned her to say that Yvonne was out of ICU. There was so much tension in their relationship that I decided to keep her mom's comment to myself.

Moments later, Yvonne awakened. She turned her head toward me. "Michael," she said, holding out her hand.

I scooted close to her. "Do you need anything?" I asked, as I reached for her hand. "How are you feeling?"

A soft smile spread across her lips. "I had an incredible experience. I saw an angel."

"What do you mean?" I asked, wondering if she was fully awake. "What are you talking about?"

> *"During the operation, something happened. An angel helped me," Yvonne said.*

Yvonne squeezed my hand. "During the operation, something happened. An angel helped me." She spoke slowly, but deliberately.

"After the surgery you were mumbling to everyone about being in heaven," I said. "Do you think you actually went to heaven?"

She tilted her head slightly and pondered my question. "More like the edge of heaven."

Yvonne proceeded to give me the details of her divine experience. I listened with my full attention. She told me about sitting on the enormous wing of an angel. She tried to describe the vivid autumn colors she saw there, but said it was difficult as the colors were more vibrant and alive than any shades she'd seen on earth.

"And Michael, love wasn't just an emotion. It was a being—God—and His presence was everywhere. It's so hard to describe, but love and peace and joy and comfort were more real there than they are here. There was no sadness. No sorrow."

As Yvonne spoke about this joyful, all-encompassing place filled with love, my mind traveled decades backward. I remembered my mother's response on the couch the moment she died. She held out her arms and a big grin spread across her face. She seemed to almost be laughing, but not at us or with us. She looked past us—almost like she was looking right through us.

Remembering how Mom's body rose up on the couch that evening, I now wondered if she saw another realm too. Maybe she saw an angel. Maybe her parents, who had passed on, were the reason she smiled. Maybe it was the joy of seeing Jesus, whom she dearly loved. I never understood Mom's reaction, but with Yvonne's explanation of her experience, it was becoming clearer.

"Besides the love there, Michael," said Yvonne, "I was shown that not only were my sins forgiven, but it was as if I never did anything wrong—like my offenses didn't exist."

As I listened to Yvonne, Psalm 103:12 popped into my mind: "As far as the east is from the west, so far has He removed our transgressions from us." It had to be because of the blood of Jesus. After all, the Bible says Christ died for our sins, but I never imagined that His sacrifice would blot out sin so permanently, so utterly.

Yvonne and I sat quietly for a moment. She was still weak and needed to rest. She closed her eyes. I slid my hand out of hers and sat back in the recliner. I was eager to hear more about her experience, but I didn't want to push.

After a few minutes, she opened her eyes again. "Something else very mysterious happened."

I leaned forward.

"I'm not sure how long I had been there, but at some point I had a tingling in my leg and I remember thinking, 'Oh, they're still working on me.' But it was like something might have gone wrong. I remember feeling like I shouldn't be able to see into both worlds the way that I could."

Chills ran down my back. My memory was transported to that moment during her surgery. I told Yvonne how I was in the waiting room and a nurse gave me updates about the procedure every fifteen or twenty minutes.

"About five hours in, I looked at my watch. It had been about thirty minutes since I heard anything, so I asked the nurse if everything was okay." I looked at Yvonne to make sure she was following my story. "The nurse said, 'I don't have any updates right now.' Then she turned the monitor away so I couldn't see what she was watching in the surgical suite."

> *The angel's voice was commanding. "The multitude is petitioning for you," he said.*

Yvonne's dark eyes opened wide.

"There's something else," she said excitedly. "Right after that, I heard the angel speak. His voice was commanding. He said: 'The multitude is petitioning for you.' I looked down to the left and could see silhouettes of people below. I had a sense they were praying for my life. But I didn't think that many people were praying—just our home group and our little church."

I leaned back in the chair and marveled. I drew in a deep breath.

"Besides our church family, I called your family in California and mine in Oregon, who put you on their mega-church prayer chains," I said. "The entire band and crew for Petra [a recording artist I managed] were praying, as well as their families. Ricky [a member of our home group who worked for Joyce Meyer] had Joyce Meyer's viewers praying for you too."

Then I told Yvonne about Jerry Bryant, who mysteriously met me at the hospital the morning of her surgery.

"Someone must have told him you were in the hospital, but I have no idea why he came to sit with me," I said. "Jerry broadcast a prayer request for you over the airwaves. Thousands of listeners! People at TBN [Trinity Broadcasting Network] put out a prayer request, and *The 700 Club* viewers offered to pray for you too."

Yvonne's eyes opened wide. "A multitude!"

I stood up and kissed her cheek.

Tears ran down her face. "I don't see myself as someone who would be worthy of that much prayer," she whispered. "I also don't know why God allowed me this wonderful gift to visit His heavenly realm and be held by an angel."

A Thin Veil

In the early evening of the day after my surgery, I was finally able to go home. I had been in the hospital for eight days. Michael walked beside me as a nurse pushed me in a wheelchair out to the car. After a week of being in a hospital, I was excited to get home to my dogs!

The physical pain was excruciating during the first two weeks. My brain was swollen and was pushing on my skull because there was simply no extra room for it—or at least that's how it felt. Ice packs on my head and regular doses of pain pills helped. Michael laid out a medication schedule on a spreadsheet to keep it all straight. He slept on the couch in the loft near our bedroom, close enough to hear me call since I needed supervision when I got out of bed because my balance was so off.

Dr. Spooner had promised me "a good headache" and was he ever right. As the painkillers wore off, it felt like my skull was going to literally explode. The searing pressure and pain was more intense than the worse migraine, and I was no stranger to headaches. Sometimes the pain was so unbearable that I'd slip off my bed and curl into a ball on the floor. I couldn't cry because it made my head hurt worse. I'd hold my face in my hands and rock back and forth. *Why did You make me come back, God? I can't bear this pain.* I often thought that my head hurt so much that I might die. I remembered a saying I once had heard: *The pain won't kill you. You only wish it would.*

> *Sometimes, when I was racked with pain, I would cry out to God, asking Him why He'd sent me back to endure this.*

But the worst of all was when I finished the steroid treatments. The pain was so torturous that I literally didn't think I would live through it. Sometimes, when I was racked with pain, I would cry out to God, asking Him why He'd sent me back to endure this. I'd always been taught that it wasn't wise to ask God "why," but I knew He loved me enough to handle my questions. The angel and God's presence remained tangibly real to me as I lay in our bed recovering day by day. I was never alone and I knew it.

I talked to the angel. *Thank you for being here. Thank you for holding me.* I was so grateful for the presence and protection. The Bible warns against worshipping angels, and I knew that no matter how glorious the angel was, it too was God's humble servant. But I found myself talking to the angel because I was still so aware of its presence. The angel was as real and as near to me as my husband, Michael.

During those first few weeks at home, I felt as if I were displaced half-way in between two worlds. Friends from church visited and brought meals while I recovered. Thankfully, Michael didn't have to worry about what we would eat for the first six weeks after I came home. I was so glad we'd moved to Tennessee. We were overwhelmed with Southern hospitality.

Late one afternoon, a woman from our home group stopped by. I was still very weak from the operation, and Michael cautioned her to only stay a few minutes as he took the casserole she'd prepared into the kitchen.

She walked into the bedroom where I lay propped up with pillows.

"The home group's been praying for you," she said cheerily. "We can't wait until you're well enough to rejoin us."

I smiled and thanked her.

"Here, I've brought you a little something."

She stepped close to my bed. She held out an eighteen-inch-tall statue.

"I was at the florist and I planned to get you a bouquet, but I saw this and thought it would be perfect!"

She put the plaster of Paris figurine on my bedside table.

"It's a garden fairy," she explained, "for your flower bed."

With a white billowing gown with pink, blue, and yellow pastel accents, the impish statue sat on its knees. The head was tilted slightly and the eyes were looking downward. It clasped its hands in front, as if praying. Remarkably, each of the large, wispy wings that protruded from its shoulders had oval-shaped holes near the tip.

"Oh, it looks like my angel," I mused.

She smiled, even though I could tell she had no idea what I was talking about. Michael came into the room.

"I'm glad you like it," she said, as she walked toward the door. "Get well soon."

I traced the oval-shaped openings on each of its wings with my fingertips. The holes were in the same place where my angel had the spot on its wing. *She bought it to remind me of the angel,* I thought in my still-fuzzy, recovering-from-brain-surgery mind.

That night, I gazed at the statue as I rested. I vividly remembered the glowing brown spot on the wing that I saw in the heavenly realm.

> *A warm knowing covered me as I realized that my guardian angel had saved me.*

My mind went back to the night my car spun out of control as I drove over the icy bridge going up to Silver Creek Falls.

A warm knowing covered me as I realized that it was my angel who had stopped the car—nothing else could have. My guardian angel had saved me.

I reminisced on other events that my angel must have experienced with me throughout the years of my life. I'd been unaware of its presence, yet there it had been, protecting me. I knew that it was doing battle for me with dark forces too.

No doubt my angel was there during some of my run-ins with my father, when I stood up for myself with an authority I didn't know I possessed. *Did my angel give me the courage? Was it the angel who spoke though me?*

What about the tumor that tried to take my life? That moment in the surgery suite when there was "trouble"? I knew for certain that my angel held me then. I experienced safety as I sat on the wing until the decision was made for me to return to my life on earth.

I thought of other situations, circumstances I'd be too ashamed for anyone to know about. My angel knew. It had been there, watching over me, guiding me to avert seen and unseen evil. I know the Lord had directed the angel to stand watch, do battle, and protect me.

Some days later, after the post-surgery fog cleared, I realized that my friend would have had no idea about my visit to heaven or my celestial guardian with the spots on its wings. But at the time, it seemed like everyone knew what my heavenly angel looked like.

I marveled at how God directed a friend from church to unwittingly bring me the perfect souvenir from my glimpse of glory. There is truly a thin veil that separates heaven from earth. I am privileged to have been able to spend time in both.

My Miracle

I'd lie in bed and try to access thoughts that now seemed to be in different "cabinets" in my mind. I'd reach for a memory that seemed to be up to the left, near the back, or another one, closer to the front, on the right, as though each had specific, literal locations in my brain. It felt like I was up inside my head at the helm and my body was a giant robot that needed to be told what to do—similar to the man behind the curtain in *The Wizard of Oz*.

Every thought was there, but it was difficult to arrange them into words. I stammered and stuttered when trying to talk about things. People who visited looked at me with pity in their eyes when I tried to explain this. One thing was crystal clear: I was not my body. The true me, the essence of my being, was only housed in this clumsy, pain-wracked, flesh-covered container. I learned that when I went to the other realm.

For several months, my short-term memory was all but nonexistent, so I often repeated myself. The telltale looks on people's faces weren't lost on me as they graciously acted like they were hearing my stories for the first time. I felt embarrassed and recited my mantra: *Sorry, I bet I already told you that, didn't I?*

Heaven forbid if someone interrupted me while I was trying to talk! Even a brief shift in the conversation made me lose focus and my train of thought. According to Dr. Spooner, this was a normal part of the recovery process for my brain. I was scheduled for my post-surgical appointment as well as follow-up appointments with MRIs every six months for the next eighteen months. If everything was fine, I'd continue with an MRI once a year, and then move on to one every two years for the rest of my life in order to monitor my recovery and the part of the tumor that was left inside.

So there I was, back in a body that wasn't capable of expressing how everything now appeared so different to me. I could recall what I'd seen and heard on the edge of heaven, but there were millions of other thoughts that I was unable to capture in words and sentences. Like a child, I was able to understand so much more than I could communicate.

I felt different, and the world looked foreign to me as if I'd never really seen it before. I yearned to write down all that I'd seen at the edge of heaven. Two weeks after I was home, I stumbled to my office for paper and a pen and climbed back into bed. Propping myself on some pillows, I set myself to the task of writing everything down. I intended to describe the beautiful angel I'd seen, but instead, I found myself writing about my unquenchable desire for the holiness I'd felt in God's presence.

It felt good to journal. I used to keep diaries as a teen to deal with the chaos in my life. I made journaling a habit throughout my recovery.

I saw Dr. Spooner for my post-surgical appointment three weeks after my surgery. I was still struggling cognitively. I felt like a newborn, partially because of my experience going to the spiritual realm and partially because my brain was still in the process of healing. A galaxy of disconnected thoughts raced through my mind. Organizing them into concepts and speech was extremely challenging.

> *A galaxy of disconnected thoughts raced through my mind. Organizing them into concepts was extremely challenging.*

Dr. Spooner greeted Michael and me in the exam room. He explained the mass was a benign meningioma, a bloody tumor that formed slowly from layers of membranes.

"How did I get it?" I asked, as I sat on the exam table.

"The causes of meningiomas vary. Predisposing factors associated with them include exposure to radiation, prolonged use of certain hormones, and sometimes genetic disorders."

I thought back to when my symptoms began, five years earlier, I started getting sick when I worked next to the server in the tiny electrical closet. I asked Dr. Spooner about it.

He shrugged his shoulders. "That would do it."

The lima-bean-sized tumor left behind in my brain would need regular follow-up MRIs to monitor it.

"If it grows or changes, we'll just zap it with a bit of radiation. It was just too risky to take it all out since the mass was wrapped around a major artery."

"I know I'll be fine," I told him with assurance. "I'm going to be one hundred percent whole again."

Dr. Spooner smiled sympathetically, but I saw doubt in his eyes. "We're still going to monitor it," he said cautiously. "I don't want you to get your hopes up."

On my second appointment six months later, I was more coherent. Dr. Spooner showed me the MRI I'd had days earlier.

He pointed a pencil at the small white spot on the film.

> *I knew something had happened with my body that had caused my soul to separate.*

"It hasn't changed, but there's always a chance it might," he said. "We'll keep watching it."

"Do tumors ever go away by themselves?" I asked.

Dr. Spooner shook his head. "Never."

He asked how I was feeling, checked my balance by having me stand with arms outstretched and eyes closed, and tested my reflexes with a rubber mallet. As our appointment was winding down, I stood beside him near the door of the exam room. I gathered my courage.

"Dr. Spooner, was there a moment that you lost me during the operation?" I asked.

I was desperately trying to put together what happened on the surgical table to cause me to visit the edge of heaven. In my heart of hearts, I knew something had happened with my body that had caused my soul to separate.

He took his hand off the doorknob and turned toward me.

"Was there a point when you lost me? Because I had an incredible experience in another reality," I said. "I was up above and saw myself sitting up on the operating table. Before surgery, I assumed I'd be lying face down."

He paused and pondered my words. His dark eyes met mine.

"Well, they gave you some pretty good drugs," he said intently.

I nodded and followed him out. I figured he wasn't open to talking about spiritual things.

A year later, I finally had my wits about me. I'd done a bit of research on the internet about near-death experiences. I wanted to know more about what had happened from Dr. Spooner's medical viewpoint. I spoke confidently with him at the end of that follow-up exam.

"I mentioned before that I'd had an incredible visit to the edge of heaven," I said. "I'm curious what anesthesia drugs I was given, and the status of my vital signs during the operation. I want to better understand the spiritual experience I had."

Dr. Spooner's mood shifted. He seemed open.

"I have heard of similar accounts like this from time to time. There isn't always an absence of vital signs when this happens," he said. "There is a lot that doctors don't understand. These experiences are outside of the realm of science and cannot be explained."

Eighteen months after the surgery, I had my third six-month follow-up MRI and appointment with Dr. Spooner. I waited on the exam table while Michael sat in a nearby chair.

After our usual greeting, Dr. Spooner's eyes shifted to the floor. My file folder was in his hand.

"Well," he raised his head and met my gaze, "I can't find it."

"What?" I exchanged a glance with Michael.

"The tumor. The part that was left behind," said Dr. Spooner. "It's not showing up on the MRI. It's not there."

"Are you saying I'm healed? That God healed me?"

Dr. Spooner smiled softly. "Well, something happened."

"Is this unusual?" I asked. "Does this ever occur?"

"No."

> *"God healed me,"*
> *I whispered in awe.*

I excitedly searched for an explanation. "Maybe my brain absorbed the fragment—could it randomly disappear?"

"No." Dr. Spooner shook his head. "That's why we often use radiation to dissolve leftover fragments."

I slid off the exam table. Michael stood beside me; his strong arms embraced me in a hug.

"God healed me," I whispered in awe. Warm tears fell from my eyes.

"Occurrences like this cannot easily be explained," he said, "but I know one thing. The tumor is no longer there."

The three of us stood in silence. Dr. Spooner closed my folder. He smiled.

"You're done. Go home!"

A Welcome Reconciliation

The years immediately following my operation were challenging. I was trying to recover physically and emotionally while, at the same time, sort out the purpose of my near-death experience and why I was sent back. I longed to know how God wanted me to use my life.

Before the surgery and my visit to the place beyond, I'd been outgoing and confident. Now I felt isolated, awkward, insecure, and timid around people. Social interaction that used to come naturally to me now felt forced.

After several months, my balance was good enough to go back to church and our home group. The overwhelming acceptance and love from the people in these groups was balm for my soul.

That first year, I had some cognitive deficits to overcome. Because of my traumatized, healing brain, I had trouble with my speech and continued to stutter as I searched for words. These difficulties existed in tandem with the gift of my near-death experience. Never before had I had such a deep understanding of my true personhood—how fully accepted I was by God. Not only was I struggling to simply communicate but my inability to put that truth into words was deeply frustrating. My body felt like a cumbersome "suit" that I was forced to wear.

Thankfully, my prayer life thrived. I no longer needed words to talk to God. I knew He heard my thoughts. I'd meditate on situations and come away with the confidence that I was heard—that God would take care of any need or request. Having a glimpse behind the veil that separates the spiritual world from this one reset my mind. For the first time, I was able to see circumstances as they truly were. One of those situations I'd struggled with my entire life was my relationship with Mom.

I'd forgiven my dad and was now ready to address all the feelings about my mother that had pent up over the years. A few months after my surgery, I started praying daily that I could forgive her.

"Father, I forgive my mom for every hurtful thing [I named all I remembered]. I repent of holding judgment against her; I know it's not my place to condemn. I pray, Father, that You would bring Your truth and healing into her life."

About six months after my surgery, a package the size of a dishwasher was delivered to the front porch. *What in the world?* I looked at the return address. *Mom.* It was so heavy that Michael had to push it over the threshold to get it inside.

He helped me pull back the flaps. Inside was a mountain of clothes. An animal print, thigh-length top with matching black leggings. A billowing Boho drop-waist dress in a paisley print. A terra-cotta hoodie. Several pair of capri-length jeans and pants. Camisoles in every color. Shirts, pants, dresses, and leggings. A dozen pairs of shoes and some handbags. All department store, designer brand, or one-of-a-kind boutique pieces.

> *I began praying that this box would provide an opening to a better relationship between us.*

I couldn't help but giggle with delight. Michael looked at me confused.

"When my kids were little, Mom sent me boxes of her hand-me-down clothes, probably once a year, but she hasn't done this in two decades," I explained.

Clothes were Mom's hobby—her passion. Gifting her clothes to me was her love language. Since we both wore the same size, she used to give me her castoffs, as well as the items she loved, if she thought they'd look particularly cute on me. A true fashionista, Mom had subscriptions to German fashion magazines when I was growing up. No one knew how to put together an outfit like my mom. And, at a petite size two, few women looked better in their clothes either.

"But why now?" I asked, as I slipped on a sapphire-colored bell-sleeved cardigan.

"Maybe it's her way of saying she's sorry?" Michael said thoughtfully. "Maybe she's appeasing her guilt."

"Guilt? For what?"

"For neglecting you when you were so sick? For not coming when you had brain surgery?" Michael suggested.

Could that be true? I began praying that this box would provide an opening to a better relationship between us.

After dinner, I picked up the phone to thank her. She excitedly described each outfit, asked me if it fit, and told me what shoes looked good with each ensemble. We talked for nearly an hour.

"It cost $80 in postage," she complained. "I won't be able to do this again. I hope you appreciate it."

I assured her I did. I thanked her over and over, not just to appease her ego, but because I was thrilled to have something "new to me." Finances were tight. What little shopping I did was from the clearance rack.

Mom and I started texting and talking on the phone several times a month. She never said she was sorry for neglecting me during my health crisis, but I knew she regretted not being there for me.

Three years later, Mom flew to Tennessee for a week. She was eighty-one. It was so good to see her, but after a couple days, I noticed she sometimes repeated herself. She put a slant on stories that seemed exaggerated or flat-out untrue. I noticed she was easily disoriented when we drove around town to go places.

A few weeks after she left our house, Mom had a mini-stroke. I could tell something was off when we talked on the phone in the weeks afterward. Several months later, she began complaining that my brother's wife was stealing from her.

I called my brother. Mom had lived in his neighborhood for more than a decade. He said she'd write checks and forget to record them in the ledger, then call the bank in an uproar. She'd make purchases on credit cards, forget what she bought, then cancel the card, saying it was fraud. She also asserted that my sister-in-law was taking family heirlooms from her house.

"Yvi, Mom's slipping," he said. "She's accusing my wife of stealing from her. She's constantly yelling and blaming her for ruining our family."

> I knew what it was like to bear Mom's wrath. But now I worried her cognitive issues were early signs of dementia.

I knew what it was like to bear Mom's wrath. She'd always been difficult, but now I worried her cognitive issues were early signs of dementia.

I began praying for her in the months after my surgery. I'd prayed to forgive. Prayed that our relationship would be reconciled. Those prayers had been answered. But now as I prayed, I felt Mom needed to be here with me.

My brother and I decided it might be best for Mom to move to Tennessee, to be near me. It took a lot of talking with Mom. She would be on board to move, then back out. She didn't want to leave California, but the tension between her and my brother's wife escalated. Well after midnight, her texts would light up my screen. *I'm all alone. I feel like everyone has thrown me away. I have no one.*

Finally in January of 2018, Michael flew out to help her pack. I picked them up at the airport. I gasped when I saw Mom.

She had gray hair that was overgrown and matted to her head. She wore no makeup. Her jacket hung off her frame. With an ashen complexion and eyes vacant from the exhausting move, she looked like a walking corpse. She was normally dressed to the nines with styled blonde hair, and I'd never seen her disheveled. On top of her careless appearance, there was a sore the size of a golf ball on her face.

Mom had always taken great pride in her appearance. She was a beautiful woman. I fought to hide my shock at seeing her this way.

She moved in with us and stayed in the guest room. It was hard. Mom was a chain-smoker, unwilling to quit. When the house across the street came up for sale, we thought she could just pay cash for it, using the money from the sale of her house in California.

In the course of trying to have her money transferred from California to Tennessee, I discovered Mom had a will and trust that was created a few years after Dad died. My brother was named trustee and beneficiary, set to inherit the entire estate upon Mom's death, except for the sum of one hundred dollars, which would go to me.

Not wanting to set her off, I approached Mom about it with measured words and guarded tone.

"How did this happen?" I asked, one morning after I made her breakfast. "How did we come to this?" It wasn't about the money, as much as the fact that she'd made arrangements to leave me out of her estate twenty years ago and I never knew about it.

She looked at me nonplussed. "Well, you never forgave your father."

"What are you talking about?" I asked. Dad had died over two decades ago. I couldn't imagine why she was bringing him up.

Mom proceeded to tell me the story Dad told her. When he drove up to San Francisco that night in 1990 to apologize, he'd returned home and told Mom and my brother that I refused to forgive him.

The memory of that wonderful visit replayed in my mind. I had no idea why in the world he would drive home and lie about what happened. Now it made sense why, in the years after his visit, they all continued to give me the cold shoulder.

I told Mom the truth of what happened that night. I'd been the family outcast for the past forty years, but here I was now, caring for my mother. None of it made sense and frankly it just didn't matter to me anymore. In order to forgive, I had to let it go. I was glad to put the past behind me. Feeling fully known and loved as I sat on the angel's wing assured me that the details of this life mattered little compared to the glory that awaited me.

> *In order to forgive, I had to let go. Feeling fully known and loved as I sat on the angel's wing assured me that the details of this life mattered little.*

One Christmas, while Michael was visiting his family in Oregon, Mom and I sat on the floor by the Christmas tree and exchanged our gifts.

"Yvilein, es ist wieder nur du und ich," she cooed, with a soft smile. "It's just you and me, again. You know how much I appreciate everything you do for me, don't you?"

My relationship with my family has been like riding a wave—you just kind of go where it takes you. Thankfully, I trust the One who created the oceans to help me hold on tight and ultimately bring me in safely.

Evidence of God

It's been more than a decade since that January morning in 2011 when I was held on an angel's wing. While many memories during the past ten years have faded, my journey to the spiritual realm remains vivid and clear—as if it happened just this morning. The experience is emblazoned in my mind more permanently than any earthly memory I have. I'm uniquely able to travel back to that divine appointment on the edge of heaven and "look around," if you will. It's as if my soul remembers every detail that happened there, rather than just my brain. I have never felt as wholly and truly alive as I did in that heavenly realm in God's presence.

Nothing, or no one, will ever convince me that what I saw, heard, and felt in that extraordinary place was not real. God graciously bestowed many gifts on me that day. As it says in Romans 8:28 (NIV): "And we know that in all things God works for the good of those who love him, who have been called according to his purpose," and I've been able to see how events that initially seemed like, or were, tragedies have come full circle to glorify God and work for my good.

Not only is the way I remember that experience profoundly different from other remembrances in my life, but my journey also impacted my view of life and how I live. If I hadn't experienced stinging rejection from family members, I wouldn't be able to understand how it grieves God when we reject Him.

As for the tumor, it's been a decade and it hasn't returned, but I'll continue to see Dr. Spooner every two years for the rest of my life. I consider it a divine appointment to be able to remind my neurosurgeon of the Great Physician who healed me after he and the surgical staff removed most of my tumor.

My hospital stay, surgery costs, and doctor bills totaled over $450,000. The benevolence fund at the hospital covered all but $700 of it. Had we not lost everything in California, or if we would have had health insurance, we'd be snowed under a mountain of debt that would take us a lifetime to repay.

My miracle healing and near-death encounter have opened the door for me to share with others. After speaking one-on-one with friends, family, and strangers God put in my path, I've spoken from the stage to church groups about my experience. Being encouraged by several people, I determined to write a book.

In spring 2017 (at fifty-nine years old), I went back to college to finish my degree in journalism and communications. In 2020, I published *Glimpse of Glory*, a book about my brain tumor, visit to the heavenly realm, miracle healing, and what I learned as a result of the ordeal.

> *My miracle healing and near-death experience have opened the door for me to share with others.*

Had I not had the experience of people doubting me, first my mom and brother and then later Michael, doctors, and friends during the five years that I suffered with mysterious symptoms associated with the tumor, I might not have been strong enough to stand firm against those who doubted the validity of my celestial encounter and how it has changed me.

Had I not been comfortable with the disbelief of others, I might have lacked the courage to continually ask Dr. Spooner for details about what happened in the operating room. Finally getting the physical answer that my vital signs dropped, coupled with his humble acknowledgment that these experiences were real and science had no answer for them, helped me make sense and substantiate what happened in my otherworldly experience.

I often didn't see evidence that God heard my prayers. I wondered if prayer really made a difference. But during my time at the edge of heaven, I saw that God really had been listening to me all along, even when there was no visible answer. I know now that every petition I'd ever offered to God had been considered. I wasn't just throwing prayers up to heaven. If I didn't receive an answer, it was because God had His reasons not to grant that petition.

I live my life with the assurance that God sees us. He hears us when we pray. He is listening. If we don't receive the answer we want, it is because God has a greater plan.

My Life since My
Near-Death Experience

Yvonne Nachtigal

The intensity of what I experienced in the celestial realm has dulled a little with time, but I go back to that place almost daily. My near-death experience profoundly affected me. I feel a new and overwhelming gratitude when I wake up each morning. This is a feeling I never want to lose—and I don't think I will.

Q *How has your NDE affected the way you see the world around you?*

A I have become aware of so many things that I was oblivious to before my surgery and before my near-death experience, like how people are strangely unaware and uninterested in what's going on around them. It's as if others are somehow tuned out to the natural world and distracted with inconsequential, useless things.

Q *Have you talked to others who have had an NDE? If so, what was that like?*

A I've spoken to two other NDE survivors and was amazed how we all very easily understood each other. It's as though we barely needed words. There is simply no vocabulary for what happened to us, which makes it so hard to describe to someone who hasn't shared the experience. But to those who have, we know. We've been there. Words aren't necessary.

❧

Q *How has your NDE affected your faith journey?*

A Perhaps the greatest revelation I received in that spiritual place was the truth that I am fully known and fully loved—that in itself is life changing. All the guilt and shame from actions that were or were not my fault during my life were lifted. The words in Isaiah 43:25 are true: "I, even I, am he who blots out your transgressions, for my own sake, and remembers your sins no more."

I always knew Christ died for the sins of the world, but to experience that reality and be shown my true spiritual identity was greater than any amount of earthly understanding. Jesus paid the price for the sins of the world on the cross. My sins were truly washed away. Finished. Final. I am literally a new creation in Him.

Since my NDE, I have no fear of not being good enough for God, of not measuring up. I know that I am who He made me to be. Being in the love and joy of God's presence has been liberating. I realize I have no need to impress, that I don't have to carefully choose words.

Of course, I need to act in accordance with His will and spread His word, but I am no longer shackled with the opinions of others or the guilt I once carried. I know I am fully loved.

❧

Q *You have always had a strong prayer life. How has that changed since your NDE?*

A I used to pray to God for something and wonder if He heard me, hoping He might answer my prayer. He didn't always answer my prayers, or He answered them in ways I didn't expect. Now I know that God answered according to His will. When I pray asking for His perfect will, I completely trust that the answer will always be the right answer, no matter what the outcome.

Making Alive Days Count

By Mark Lalli, as told to Stephanie Thompson

The tests of life are not to break you but to make you.

Norman Vincent Peale

M y combat boots stomped a cadence across the linoleum floor of the crew chief's office that cold morning on November 8, 2007. A United States Army aviation soldier stationed at an Italian air force base, I was getting ready to accompany a subordinate to a promotion review board meeting.

My platoon sergeant stuck his head out of his office.

"Hey, Lalli, you gotta fly," said SFC (Sergeant First Class) Berry, in a matter-of-fact tone.

He explained that a joint mission air training flight was scheduled with members of the US Air Force in a couple of hours. He wanted the senior crew chief with the most experience to go. That was me.

"We want to show them our stuff. I need my best people on the flight for this dog and pony show."

I nodded. "You got it, Sarge."

I hurried back to my apartment and jumped into my flight suit, scarf, and overcoat. I'd be in someone else's Black Hawk helicopter today, since mine was at the US Army base in Germany having a routine maintenance inspection.

Little did I know that a noncombat mission would change my life forever.

Heritage of the Military

The legacy of military service in my family dates all the way back to the American Revolution. It was my dream to continue that proud tradition—to follow in my ancestors' footsteps. My father's shoulder issues kept him from joining the service, but both my grandfathers were military men who enlisted after the bombing of Pearl Harbor during World War II. All I ever wanted was to become a soldier.

As a preschooler, I loved playing with my Ertl miniature die-cast helicopters, fighter jets, trucks, tanks, and jeeps. I had a full airbase of mobile military vehicles that I positioned around my bedroom. I'd crawl on my knees through the carpeting, toys in hand. For hours, I'd entertain myself as I imagined plotlines for enemy invasions and American victories.

I'm sure my obsession had something to do with the era in which I lived. Born in 1985, I was five years old when Operation Desert Shield began. Whenever a news report about combat in Operation Desert Storm flashed on the television, I'd stand at attention, mesmerized by the pictures of soldiers charging across the sand in their tan-and-brown camouflage. I was too young to understand the words that the reporters spoke, and I didn't have an inkling about the possible deadly consequences the invasion entailed. All I knew was what I saw on the screen—airplanes, tanks, jeeps, and high-ranking soldiers boasting about certain victories.

As the Gulf War continued to rage on, my G.I. Joe action figure and I played "war," hiding behind hedges around the backyard of our house. I carried out secret missions for the two of us. I yearned for the day I could become a real-life G.I. Joe, but until then, I enjoyed my predictable, safe, middle-class existence in the midwestern United States, where I lived with my parents and my brother, Peter, who was five years older.

My Grandpa Nick, my mom's dad, lived close to us. He was my constant companion and was very special to me. He'd come over to visit and sometimes stayed a week or two at our house. He was an eager playmate and showered me with lots of attention.

Besides my fascination with the Gulf War and Grandpa Nick, there was little about my upbringing that would have pointed me toward an interest in the miltary.

An artilleryman in WWII, Grandpa Nick participated in five invasions in the Pacific. I couldn't get enough of his stories and asked loads of questions: "Did you get shot at? What was it like to fire the cannons?" Even at such a young age, I found his military history fascinating.

Sometimes when I knew he was coming to visit, I begged Mom to ask him to bring his leather-bound scrapbook filled with pictures of the people he served with and newspaper clippings detailing the war. The front page of the *Santa Fe New Mexican* on V-J day was my favorite.

Grandpa Nick and I spent a lot of time together during those five years before he died. It happened in the summer before I started third grade. I was devastated to lose him.

Besides my fascination with the Gulf War and Grandpa Nick, there was little about my upbringing that would have pointed me toward an interest in the military. My brother and I never shot guns, hunted, camped in the wilderness, or vacationed in rustic places like a cabin or lodge. Despite the history of military service in my family, there was nothing outdoorsy about us, except perhaps the country music I liked to listen to on the radio.

About the most backwoods activity Pete and I did was kayaking or canoeing on the Wading River when our family drove back East to spend time with my paternal grandparents, who lived in rural New Jersey.

The eight-hour drive from Ohio to visit them each summer took us through several states, including West Virginia. Decades before smartphones, Pete and I slept in the backseat or looked out the car windows. I couldn't help but notice the pastoral landscapes, rolling hills, and beautiful trees. Very different from the topography of Strongsville, our Ohio suburb.

I wanted to "be all that I could be," just like the army commercial said.

The summer between my fourth- and fifth-grade years, my family went to Washington, DC. We took in all the familiar sightseeing destinations, including touring the White House and the Smithsonian's National Air and Space Museum.

But what stood out most for me was Arlington National Cemetery. At the Tomb of the Unknown Soldier, I watched a white-gloved military sentinel in full dress blues stand at attention while two others marched precisely in unison as they patrolled the concourse, shiny brown rifles slung over their shoulders. The way they moved and carried themselves left an indelible impression on me. I could see myself doing that very same thing one day.

Every time the army commercial "Be All You Can Be" played on the radio or television, I couldn't help but remember the precise movements of the soldiers at the Tomb of the Unknown Soldier as well as the brave warriors who ran across the desert. I wanted to do what they were doing. I wanted to be all I could be too.

A Life of Service

Military service wasn't the only activity that appealed to me. I loved serving at our church too.

We attended St. Matthew's Episcopal Church in Brecksville, Ohio, every Sunday. I was an acolyte from the time I was eight until I was eighteen. After getting to church about thirty minutes early Sunday mornings, I dressed in my robe and helped the priest get ready for the service. My first duty was being a torchbearer. During the opening procession, I carried a long wooden stick with a lighted candle as I walked the aisle with our priest, Father Alan James, and another acolyte who carried an oversized Bible.

At the altar, I lit the other candles and took my seat on stage until it was time to assist Father by holding a candle when he read the gospel from the large leather-bound Bible. I liked having a job to do, feeling important. A natural extrovert, I also liked being part of the show. Playing a part in the worship was a way I served not only my church family, but God too.

Relatively young, in his midforties, and popular with the youth, Father Alan, as he was known to us, had served in the navy before he came to our parish. He was relatable and empathetic. I admired the way he cared about the congregation and the way he spoke to people. Some priests would talk down to us, preach at us, especially the youth group, but that wasn't Father Alan's style.

After the message, he'd invite the children to the altar. He'd sit on the step and they circled around him while he explained the sermon in words that we all could understand. He was a true example of Christ. He had a servant's heart and never projected himself as though he were above anyone. Even though I was too old to sit on the steps, I appreciated hearing the sermon truths spoken in plain language.

> *The organizational rituals of the Episcopal Church inspired me.*

Between the sermon and communion, one of the deacons would come forward to the altar and offer prayers. While the congregation knelt in the pews, he'd read the names of people who needed prayer—the president, our church leaders, and our governor. Then he'd read off the names of people in peril, the old, infirmed, and injured who needed us to intercede for them too.

Toward the end, he'd ask for the prayers of the people. The congregants could pray silently, or say out loud the names of those individuals for whom they were interceding. After each name was spoken, the congregation said in union: *Hear our prayer.*

The organizational rituals of the Episcopal Church inspired me. We stood to worship, sat to learn, and knelt to pray. After the Prayers of the People, I rose from my kneeling position and took my place to help during communion, holding the holy water while the priest washed his hands, carrying the chalice with the wine, or offering the plate of the communion wafers.

Father Alan was also very involved with our youth group. He was always around to give his quiet guidance when we asked. Once I got to high school, I took a leadership position as the head of the acolytes. It was my job to instruct and mentor the younger kids. I modeled Father Alan's patience and understanding ways as I taught them to serve.

I liked being a good example and a positive role model. Helping in the church and being beneficial to others was the way I honored God—my service was the cornerstone of our relationship. In my serving, I felt like I was pleasing God. I always felt close to Him.

Somewhere along the way, I formed the belief that heaven was a reward for doing good and following God. I tried hard to do the right thing and be my best self.

One fall morning during my sophomore year of high school, my class was outside playing softball when I noticed a low-flying plane.

"Look," I pointed skyward. The whole class saw it.

Not long after, we heard about the terrorists and the four plane crashes they caused. A strange realization dawned on me. I was certain that the plane we saw outside was United Airlines Flight 93 that crashed into a field in Pennsylvania.

The events of September 11, 2001, touched me deeply. I watched first responders on the television news reports—firefighters, police officers, paramedics, all running in and out of the Twin Towers, risking their lives. A thought inside my head stirred: *These enemies are going to be with us for a while. We all need to step up. Why not me?* I thought.

Becoming a Soldier

A month later, I went to talk to Sergeant Krause, a US Army recruiter who visited my high school weekly. My best friend, PJ, and I brought our lunches into the career room so we could spend time with him while we ate.

After a couple months, I mentioned my interest in the military to Dad.

"Hey, I've been thinking about joining the army," I said one weekend while we watched a game on television.

He shook it off. "Sure. When you get out of college, you can go."

But the army recruiter had armed me with information during all those lunch meetings.

"Actually, I can sign up for the reserves once I turn seventeen," I explained. "When I graduate high school, I'll already be enlisted and I can start my job training."

Dad eyed me cautiously. "How do you know that?"

I told him about Sgt. Krause and how I'd spent my lunch hours with him over the past few months.

Dad might have been guarded about the topic, but when I told Mom, she totally freaked out.

"Your father and I need to talk to this guy," she said, her brows knitted with worry. "What if he's telling you a bunch of lies?"

A few weekends later, Sgt. Krause came to our house for lunch. He explained how I could go to basic training next summer, between my junior and senior years of high school. He promised I wouldn't see combat until I graduated and was trained for duty.

Mom still wasn't sold, but both my parents knew it was in my heart to enlist. I also talked to Father Alan, who encouraged me to pray and seek God's will.

"I want to get outside the fish tank," I told him one day when we talked at youth group. "I want to see what's out there."

Many people in our town were born here and stayed here. I wanted more. I wanted to see the world!

Father Alan had known me for most of my life. He said he'd pray for me, too, and support me, no matter what path in life I chose.

A year later, in November 2002, Mom, reluctantly, and Dad signed a waiver to allow me to join the US Army Reserve the week after my seventeenth birthday. They gave me the best gift I could have had. It was my first step in claiming the adventuresome life I'd always yearned for—a life as a soldier.

> *I wanted to save people, to be that kind of guy—a righteous soldier.*

I spent the summer between my junior and senior year in basic training at Fort Sill, Oklahoma. When I got to boot camp in that hot, dry place, the majority of my time was filled with running in one-hundred-degree weather wearing a full uniform.

Days later, the drill sergeant handed me a toothbrush, but it wasn't for my teeth. On my hands and knees, I cleaned the toilets, scrubbing hard with that toothbrush. I also was tasked with waxing the floors in our barracks, sometimes up to five times a day. The senseless acts irritated me. *Is this really what I signed up for?*

Where were the soldiers from Desert Storm that I saw on the nightly news? Those warriors used cool equipment and drove tanks through the sand. They took out the bad guys, helped the oppressed, and toppled inhuman regimes. I wanted to do what they did. I wanted to save people, to be that kind of guy—a righteous soldier.

My last year of high school, I had an awful case of senioritis. I couldn't wait to leave Strongsville and my mundane life behind.

Thankfully, basic training gave me a newfound maturity to do what I needed to do and to always do my best. I went to the armory for training drills once a month. I studied harder than I ever had in school, making a 4.0 my senior year.

My ceramics teacher, Mrs. Pusti, heard that I had enlisted. After school one day, I stopped by her art room.

"I want to give you this good luck medallion," she said.

I smiled. Mrs. Pusti was one of my favorite teachers. I turned the silver coin over in my hand. On one side was an angel.

> I signed up for a six-year commitment as a Black Hawk mechanic. I'd loved helicopters from the time I could crawl. It seemed like a perfect fit.

"Bring it back to me when you come home," she said, her blue eyes shining behind her glasses.

After graduating high school in May of 2004, I went active duty. I scored high in mechanics on my aptitude test and signed up for a six-year commitment as a Black Hawk mechanic. I always liked to tinker with things, and I'd loved helicopters from the time I could crawl. It seemed like a perfect fit.

I went for my job training in Fort Eustis, Virginia, from August through November of 2004. I learned how to review the repair manuals for the aircraft and how to make the warranted repairs.

In town one afternoon, I stopped by a jewelry store and saw a St. Michael medal. St. Michael the Archangel is the patron saint of people who work in dangerous conditions, like soldiers and aviators. I already had a St. Christopher medal that I always carried with me, along with the good luck coin from Mrs. Pusti and a rosary. Since there was a war going on, I figured I'd need all the help I could get. I purchased the silver St. Michael medal with a picture of the archangel, his sword drawn and foot on the neck of the devil on one side and the patron saint's prayer on the other.

After I finished job training in Virginia, I was stationed at Fort Hood in Texas.

On a midtour leave, I went home to Ohio for a couple weeks. PJ was home from college too. One day we went to a tattoo shop. I pulled my shiny St. Michael medal out of my pocket.

"I want this," I said, showing the artist my religious medallion. "Can you do this?"

It took a couple of hours, but when he finished, I had a six-inch replica of the patron saint of soldiers on my left bicep. I smiled as I inspected the impressive image. St. Michael perfectly symbolized good prevailing over evil, my faith in God, and my devotion to being a soldier.

Multiple Deployments

In December 2005, I boarded a huge commercial aircraft with hundreds of other soldiers from Fort Hood. We were headed to the Middle East. As I buckled my seat belt, I took out my St. Michael medal. I looked at the fierce archangel for a moment before turning the round coin to the prayer printed on the flip side. Silently, I read the prayer that I'd now memorized:

St. Michael the Archangel, defend us in battle, be our defense against the wickedness and snares of the devil; may God rebuke him, we humbly pray, and do thou, O Prince of the heavenly hosts, by the divine power of God, thrust into hell Satan and all the evil spirits who prowl about the world seeking the ruin of souls. Amen.

I zipped it into a rectangular coin purse that held my St. Christopher medal, rosary, and Mrs. Pusti's good luck coin, then slid it into my pocket for the fifteen-hour flight.

Having been promoted several times, I was being deployed to Iraq as a UH-60 crew chief. The Utility Helicopter (UH) Black Hawk was a four-blade, twin-engine, medium-lift helicopter designed for the utility transport of people, food, weapons, or animals.

I often joked that being a crew chief was a mix between a NASCAR pit crew member and a glorified flight attendant.

As a crew chief, it was my job to make sure everything was good to go for the aircraft to complete its assignment. On every mission, I did preflight and post-flight checks for many things—to make sure the instrument panel was working properly, to gauge if the engine was burning fuel efficiently, and other things. I reviewed the logbook to look for inspections that were due or any notes regarding previous flights.

Not only were crew chiefs responsible for repairing the aircraft and getting it ready for missions, but we also went up during the flight in the birds, as we called them. Once in the sky, I was responsible for every-thing that happened behind the pilot's seats—cargo and people. It was an important position, and with the various duties I performed, I often joked that being a crew chief was a mix between a NASCAR pit crew member and a glorified flight attendant.

We landed in Kuwait at a very different type of base than the one I'd become accustomed to. Instead of barracks that were buildings, our encampment consisted of hundreds of huge tents.

Surprisingly, it was cold and wet—snow flurries fell from the sky the evening we landed. The plan was to acclimate to the cold nights and hot days in the desert and then finish our training for a month or so before receiving our combat assignments and moving north into Iraq.

Once our aircrafts were shipped in, it was up to us crew chiefs to repair, service, and ready them for flight. We practiced performing landings and the proper strategies for landing in the desert sands. We trained on operations to test our weapons by shooting targets that were placed throughout the desert.

Crew chiefs are part of the flight crew in peacetime and in combat, but in combat, we hold a secondary responsibility as door gunners. In Iraq, I would multitask as a door gunner, positioned to guard, protect, and defend crew and cargo. A heavy-duty machine gun was mounted on the window beside me. My hand was always in the ready position to keep my fellow soldiers safe and the perimeter protected, and also to defend our bird and equipment.

Christmas in Kuwait held no gift exchanges, but our platoon sergeant gave us each a flashlight. A few days later, we were scheduled to jump north to Taji, Iraq. The night before we were to go into Iraq, I lay on my cot. Surrounded by rows of a hundred other men in a giant tent that was our makeshift barracks, I knew I needed to get some sleep, but the reality of what I was about to experience kept me awake. I wasn't a life-sized G.I. Joe action figure. This wasn't a promotional videotape or the nightly news on television of some far-off battlefield. This was my life. I could very well lose it.

As I thought about going into a war zone, a scene from the book *Band of Brothers* played through my mind. I remembered how one of the characters made a promise to God: "If You see me through D-Day and this war, I'll be a good person, the kind of person who publicly does good and serves others."

I decided to make that deal. If it worked for him, it would work for me too. As I stared at the tent pole overhead, I struck a bargain with the Almighty.

God, if You see me through this year in Iraq, I will be better. I will do good. I'll help people. I'll move forward. I'll do good in the community. Please God, keep me safe. Let me stay alive.

The next day, the 3rd Battalion, 4th Aviation Regiment of the 4th Infantry Division made the five-hour flight to Taji, our camp for our tour of duty. I was assigned to a sixty-person platoon with pilots, Black Hawk mechanics, and other crew chiefs like me.

When 2006 rolled in, I was on the flight line at our base in Iraq when ear-popping explosions sounded around me.

Instead of a fireworks display that sometimes accompanies celebrations to ring in the New Year, the Iraqi soldiers in war zones fired their guns in the air. It was a chilling reminder that I wasn't in the United States anymore.

Our main mission was to fly air assaults. Four or five helicopters caravanned at a time. We'd pick up a unit of soldiers under the cover of darkness, in the hours between sundown and midnight, and drop them behind enemy lines.

Twenty-four or forty-eight hours later, depending on the mission, we'd swoop down and pick them up. Sometimes we rendezvoused in a field. Sometimes it was a river. Sometimes it was just outside the city, a block or so from the fighting.

Similar to limo security a famous rock star might have, we served as a sort of a Black Hawk taxi service for combat soldiers. All kidding aside, it was quite dangerous. Everything about Operation Iraqi Freedom was perilous.

Our area of operation was Baghdad and the ten miles north and south of the city. We flew all hours of the day, but primarily at nighttime, when we could be less visible. The darkness also provided a great reprieve from the sweltering summer temperatures that could reach upwards of a hundred and ten degrees during the daytime. Amazingly, nighttime in the desert got down to the fifties and sixties—a crazy temperature swing.

It was rare to fly with the same people on the same aircraft every single time. In America, we flew with the same crew, but here it didn't matter, as we all knew each other pretty well from our time serving together at Fort Hood.

Reality struck. I started counting. Soldiers getting off our birds, soldiers getting back on—the numbers never matched.

At first, I was excited to be doing the job I trained for. It was an honor to bring people in and get them out safely. But the hours were long. Our flight crew took ten- to twelve-hour shifts. We'd be off eight hours and then back at it.

After a week, a strange knowing covered me. Reality struck. I started counting.

I'd count how many soldiers we loaded onto our helicopters and dropped in the middle of the fighting. When we came back to pick them up the next day, I counted again. Soldiers getting off our birds, soldiers getting back on—the numbers never matched.

Sometimes, I would rack my brain, trying to remember faces. Trying to remember who it was that jumped out and ran into the darkness. *Who was it that didn't come back?* Try as I might, the faceless, fatigue-wearing soldiers all melted together. And I couldn't help but feel responsible for delivering them to a certain death.

Another of our routine missions entailed flying fallen soldiers to the airport so their remains could be transported to their loved ones in the states. Hero Missions—that's what we called them. Young men and women, much like me, who had lost their lives serving their country.

The only way to get through my duty was to dissociate—I numbly moved through the motions, did my job, and tried not to think too much.

Loading the black body bags onto individual stretchers weighed heavily on me. These were my brothers and sisters in arms. *It's not how it's supposed to be.* The army called them "prized heroes," but none of us envied their status.

My pride was mixed with deep sadness and overwhelming despair. On one hand, I was proud that we were getting the fallen soldiers home to their families. But oftentimes when I lifted a light stretcher, I could tell there was very little that remained.

The only way to get through my duty was to dissociate—I numbly moved through the motions, did my job, and tried not to think too much. I survived my yearlong tour in Iraq. I made it out without physical injuries, but the emotional damage from living in a war zone had taken its toll.

On leave back home in Ohio after our combat tour of duty ended, I surprised Mrs. Pusti. The principal let me sneak into her art room in the middle of class. As I turned the doorknob, she looked my way. Tears sprang from her eyes and dripped down her cheeks as she stood to greet me.

I took her lucky coin out of my pocket and pressed it in her hand.

"You told me to bring it back to you," I whispered. "I made it through Iraq."

She wrapped her arms around me and hugged me tight.

Exciting Europe

My next assignment was a noncombat stay at Aviano Air Base in Italy. Because of our specialization with aircrafts, our company of aircraft pilots, mechanics, and other personnel was stationed at the air force base, even though we were US Army soldiers.

I had the time of my life in Europe! History had been my favorite subject in school, and here I was in the birthplace of the Renaissance. My apartment was a forty-five minute train ride from Venice to the base. I loved riding in the gondolas, wandering around St. Mark's Square, and visiting the Basilica. I sent postcards home as I'd sightsee in Verona, Italy, a medieval old town built between the meandering Adige River—famous for being the setting of Shakespeare's *Romeo and Juliet*. While in England, France, and Spain, I saw landmarks like the Eiffel Tower, La Sagrada Familia Cathedral, Big Ben, the Crown Jewels, and the London Tower Bridge.

Most weekends, I'd wander up and down the canal and enjoy myself while taking in all the history as a tourist. I rode the train to Florence too. When it came time for my vacation, I had two weeks leave, and PJ joined me from the States. We went from Venice to Florence, then to Pisa, Milan, Barcelona, Paris, and London and then back to Italy. I embraced the opportunity to live in the birthplace of Western civilization. I marveled at buildings that were centuries old. It was a great big world and I couldn't wait to see all of it!

I'd seen atrocities on the battlefield and it changed me. I felt deeply disenchanted with the way of war, the losses I encountered—horrible deaths of young soldiers, soldiers like me. It was my helicopter that took them into battle, and I felt guilty for those we pulled aboard who were badly wounded—or who didn't make it back.

> *Overwhelming helplessness at not being able to protect the soldiers haunted me.*

Overwhelming helplessness at not being able to protect them haunted me. After all, I helped deliver them to their fate by dropping them off behind enemy lines. It didn't make sense, but I felt deeply responsible.

Somehow in all of it, I blamed God too. I was angry. *If You care and love us so much, how can You allow this to happen?* I witnessed American soldiers brutally killed, tortured, and beheaded by the Iraqis—and for what? We were there to help those people. To free them from an evil dictator and a radical regime.

I tried to push it all down, to keep those dark thoughts deep inside my mind. After all of my running and gunning in Iraq, the downtime in Europe was a blessing. The pace was slow and my mission was easy. I was a professional military man, but I was also a young adult, a twenty-one-year-old kid. Sometimes my buddies and I drank too much or drove too fast, to let off a little steam. I was reckless many times, like climbing mountains without a rope or going places and not letting anyone else know where I was going. Deep down I think that's the way I coped with the wartime tragedies.

Then, on Cinco de Mayo weekend of 2007, I met a girl in an Italian pub. Jess was Australian, living in London. She told me how the UK and Australia had a program to allow their citizens to live in either country without visas, so she was in London working and traveling around Europe. Fun-loving Jess seemed as adventuresome as I. We started talking online.

One evening while we Skyped, an idea popped into my mind.

"Hey, you know, I'm going to be in Paris next weekend. If you want to meet me, you can follow me back. We could hang out in Italy."

So she did. Jess came back to Italy with me.

"Well, why don't you just stay at my place?" I made enough money to feed us and even though I had a one-bedroom apartment, I didn't mind sleeping on the couch for a time.

Jess moved in. A month later, I got new orders. That July, I left for a three-month, noncombat, joint-training mission with the US and Romanian armies. I was scheduled to be back at the end of September.

I said goodbye to Jess and packed my bags for the multimonth mission. I'd been out of Iraq for six months. Out of the six of us crew chiefs and medics, five of us had only been out of a combat zone for less than a year. Besides our footlockers and duffel bags, we brought a lot of emotional baggage with us on the mission.

The conditions in Romania were dreadful. We worked ten- to fourteen-hour days, with little time off. Our living quarters were two-man trailers, reminiscent of the ones we stayed in during combat. After a few weeks, we were on each other's nerves due to the stress of the mission.

Because most of us had recently been in a combat zone, we struggled from undiagnosed mental health issues like PTSD and depression. In Italy, we were happy, so the issues didn't surface as often, but the mental and emotional fatigue from working so much caused our emotions and behaviors to sometimes be erratic.

We'd been in Romania for two months when our exercise commander called a chaplain from Germany in an attempt to get us some emotional help.

"See how we're living here?" I said to the chaplain. "In trailers, unable to leave this old, run-down, Soviet air base—working around the clock. We're living like we're in a combat zone, but not getting imminent danger pay or any added benefits."

He tried to console us, but we knew he had no power to get us out of there. All he could do was listen to us and pray.

For the first time in my life, prayer didn't matter to me. I was far from God.

The mission dragged on, but a few weeks into October we were scheduled to leave. We were to fly back to Italy on Tuesday, but because of adverse weather conditions, flights over the Alps got bumped. Tuesday turned into Wednesday, then Thursday, and then Friday, and we still couldn't leave. We were all sick of it—not so much the weather, but of being overworked and living in the poor conditions amid the pointlessness of being there. We just wanted to go back to Italy.

About 6 p.m., a group of us wandered down to the base canteen, a little shop that provided free beer. It was nothing fancy, basically a bucket full of iced beer stuck outdoors with music playing from a boom box inside.

After a few drinks, my buddies were ready to make the five-minute walk back to the trailers. Thunderstorms were in the forecast, and they wanted to get back before the rain, but I stayed. It was just as well that they left, because in addition to everything else that was going on, we'd all grown weary of being around each other constantly. I felt irritated, annoyed, and angry with some of them—maybe all of them.

But it was more than frustration. I loved my job. I loved serving. But the fantasy life I'd created growing up watching army television commercials and Stormin' Norman on the nightly news was far from reality. The army slogan "Be All You Can Be" might have hooked me as a kid, but I couldn't help thinking that there had to be more. More for me.

I wasn't just frustrated with the army, our mission, my bunkmates, and myself. I was mad at God.

After a few more beers, I headed toward the trailers, a Budweiser beer bottle in hand. The moon lit my way as I staggered over the ground. In the distance, I could see a storm rolling in over the Black Sea. Feelings of irritation replayed in my mind. I felt stuck.

Suddenly, thunder clapped loudly and a huge bolt of lightning danced across the ebony sky. I realized I wasn't just frustrated with the army, our mission, my bunkmates, and myself. I was still mad at God.

"Well, You caused that, so how about this?" I screamed, as I threw the empty bottle against a concrete retaining wall in front of me. I watched it shatter into a hundred pieces.

"You call this a storm?" I yelled, words slurring. "I'll give You a storm. I don't think You are who You say You are. Prove to me that You're real. Prove to me You're God."

All the emotions I'd pushed down since Iraq gushed up. I knew my temper tantrum wasn't really so much about God as it was the helplessness and unhappiness I felt. Tears rolled down my face as the rain pounded down on me. I cursed and shuffled my feet back to my bunk.

Ever since Iraq, I knew I was not in a good place, but instead of doing something to care for myself, I tried to forget about what I had seen, what I had done. My risk-taking behavior subconsciously dared God to intervene. To show me that He truly existed.

I was in a very dark place.

A Deadly Malfunction

A week and a half later, I was back in Italy at Aviano Air Base. One of my subordinates was going up before the promotion review board, and I wanted to speak on his behalf. I always was glad to help deserving soldiers rank up.

Even though I'd just turned twenty-two a couple of days earlier, I'd been promoted five times. I guess you could say I'd come up through the ranks quickly. As a flight instructor, it was my job to train all the new crew chiefs and to ensure the trained crew chiefs maintained the correct standard for their job.

"Don't mention your age to anyone," my supervisor warned. "You're younger than everyone else you're in charge of and training."

The morning of November 8, 2007, my platoon sergeant found me in the crew chief office.

"Hey, Lalli, you gotta fly," said SFC Berry.

He explained that an air force unit chief saw we had a routine flight that day. They had an airman who was reenlisting and wanted to do a reenlistment ceremony in the air on our bird.

We regularly had training flights like this. We needed to fly a certain number of hours every month to maintain our status, experience, and knowledge of the aircraft. When we knew this flight was going to go off, our flight schedule was published with all branches of service since everyone needed to know by whom, and when, the airspace was being used. We relished having the chance to show other branches of service how cool our army jobs were and how much fun we had on the Black Hawk.

We relished having the chance to show other branches of service how cool our army jobs were.

Sgt. Berry put his hand on my shoulder. "I need our most experienced crew chief to show them our best stuff."

"You got it!" I said with a wink.

I looked at my watch. The mission was at 09:30. That left me with about an hour to change, get back, and inspect the aircraft.

We had four Black Hawk helicopters in the company. Sarge knew that my aircraft, the one that I was responsible for, had flown on our mission to Romania. On the way back to Italy the previous week, we had dropped it at our German Army base for routine maintenance.

"You're flying Duke '00," he added.

I nodded. We had names for all the Black Hawk helicopters, and today I'd fly in another crew chief's bird. Occasionally crew chiefs switched aircrafts, but not often. Still, it was nothing out of the ordinary. Nothing to be concerned with. I didn't give it a second thought.

I apologized to my subordinate and arranged for someone else to accompany him. I hurried back to my apartment, put on my flight suit, scarf, and overcoat. I carefully unzipped my right chest pocket and slipped in my black rectangular coin purse that contained my St. Christopher medal, the rosary, and my St. Michael medal, then said goodbye to Jess.

At the hanger, I flipped through the preflight log and made sure there were no inspections coming up. I checked the weather report—chilly, but great conditions for flying. Everything looked perfect on paper. I moved on to my visual inspection of the craft.

> *I checked the weather report—chilly, but great conditions for flying. Everything looked perfect on paper.*

The sky was deep blue that Thursday morning. Our two pilots arrived and we went over the itinerary. We'd spend a little over an hour and a half in the air.

Moments later, eight soldiers from the US Air Force introduced themselves and climbed into the back of the aircraft.

I started my monologue—my flight attendant safety regulation speech, as I liked to call it.

"Hi, I'm Sgt. Lalli. I'm the crew chief. Your pilots today are Captain Skoglund and CW2 Alvarez. We'll be flying through the Piave Training Area, following the Piave River and showing you how we fly in combat situations. At times, we'll be flying close to the ground, as well as making some slope landings, and pulling some hard turns. If you should feel like you're going to get sick, throw up in your helmet or in your shirt. I don't like cleaning it up at the end of the flight. Always keep your seat belt on. If we should need to make a hard landing, stay in your seats with your seat belt fastened. Continue to sit up straight with your feet on the ground. Listen to the crew for all instructions. In the event of an emergency, we have fire extinguishers on board. Now I'll check and make sure your seat belts are properly secured."

I watched the soldiers buckle into their five-point safety harnesses, making sure each was fastened. I sat on my bench, buckled into my safety harness, and strapped on my helmet with a built-in microphone and headset to communicate with the pilots, who sat beside each other in the front of the craft.

My seat was aligned directly behind the pilots, but the back of my seat faced sideways. My back was facing the inside of the aircraft so that as crew chief I could monitor activity out the window and keep my eyes on the airmen who sat on three horizontal benches in the middle and back of the chopper. It was a little cramped, but there was enough room to fit.

We lifted off and climbed into the sky, bumping along like a roller coaster through the valleys, over the river, and between the mountains. The pilots were pushing the aircraft to its limits to demonstrate what it was made to do. I watched the airmen's faces. They were all smiles, laughing along as we took a joyride through the cloudless sky.

The pilots made hairpin turns, spins, and dips. We flew backward and forward. We'd been in the air almost an hour and a half and were nearing the end of the mission. We were about twenty-two miles southwest of Aviano Air Base, over the Piave River on the outskirts of the small town of Santa Lucia di Piave, when the pilot called the base for clearance to fly home.

The aircraft shuddered ever so slightly. I thought I heard something bang. Of course, I had a helmet on. It was impossible to hear anything like that up there with the roar of the engines and rush of wind noise. Still...

The helicopter started spinning.

Oh my God! No!

At first, our passengers thought it was part of the ride. But the faster we descended, their screams of joy turned to cries of terror.

"Hey, are you going to stop this?" I said into my headset to the pilots.

"I can't," one of them said, panic rising. "I can't stop it."

Dread washed over me. I looked out the window. We spun madly toward the earth. I could see we were in a field, near a dry riverbed. I turned to the passengers in the back. I tried to calm them, ease their minds, but I was terrified myself. My heart felt like it had dropped into the pit of my stomach, as I knew what was about to happen.

We'd passed the point of no return. Disaster was imminent. We were going to crash.

We'd passed the point of no return. Disaster was imminent. We were going to crash. I felt helpless, but I had to exude confidence. Keep the passengers calm. For their sake.

I put my hands in the air.

"It's okay," I said, nodding my head, as if that would convince them. "We're going to be all right."

I tried to ease their minds and keep everybody calm like a flight attendant on a commercial plane would, but my trepidation soared as our helicopter descended.

"You'll be fine." I nodded encouragingly. "We'll all be fine."

I had to be brave for them, but deep down I knew we wouldn't be okay. Not anything close to okay. In fact, the likelihood of any of us surviving was slim.

As the helicopter plummeted wildly toward the ground, I glimpsed horror in the eyes of the airmen. I wondered if my eyes looked like that too.

Stop! Stop! Stop! The thought shrieked inside my mind as the bird dropped downward two hundred feet through the sky.

Out the window, I glimpsed the riverbed below. The ground was rushing close fast. We were going to hit the dirt at a force of more than 50 Gs.

Dear God! Help us!

A Mother's Fear: Is Mark Hurt?

That Thursday morning, my neighbor Nancy and I sat at my kitchen table chatting over a cup of coffee. She and her family lived down the block. We'd been good friends since the day we met at the school bus stop when Mark and her daughter were kindergartners. Nancy had stopped by to pick up theater tickets I'd gotten for her, when a friend from church called.

"Ann, what's the name of the base where Mark is stationed?" Carolyn asked.

I told her it was Aviano Air Base in Italy.

"Okay," she said slowly. "My husband saw something on the internet about a helicopter crash in Italy. They are reporting that it's an American army unit from Germany. They're near some town that starts with a T. I'm sorry, but I can't remember the name of the town."

"Treviso," I offered, cautiously. Mark was stationed near Treviso, Italy.

"Yes, that's it," she said.

My stomach sank as I hung up the phone. Thankfully Nancy was there at the house with me. We went to the computer and found the news story online. The details were sketchy. No names were mentioned.

I pulled my cell phone out of my purse and dialed Mark's mobile number. It went straight to voice mail. My breath caught. Getting his voice mail that quickly meant that he'd shut off his phone. The only time Mark turned off his phone was when he was flying. I gathered my composure so I could leave a message.

"Hi, Mark. It's Mom." I tried to hold my voice steady and sound casual. "We saw there was a helicopter accident. Give me a call when you can so I know you're okay."

I looked at the clock. With the five-hour time difference, Mark would have already finished lunch. The crash happened a couple hours ago. If Mark were not involved, surely he would have thought to call and let us know he was safe.

Nancy grabbed my hand. "I'm sure he's fine."

A few minutes later, I tried his cell phone again. *Please, God, let him answer.* It went straight to voice mail.

Dread bubbled up. Mark had made it through a year in the combat zone of Iraq unscathed. Our parish offered prayers each day for his safety. Many people were still praying for him, as they did for all our soldiers who grew up in the church.

I shook my head. The likelihood of him being in an accident now was slim. That's what I told myself, at least. And that's what I heard myself say to Nancy. But the longer I waited for news, the more fearful I became.

My husband, Rich, was working out of town that week. Thank goodness for Nancy.

"I'm going to stay with you awhile," she said. "Just until we hear that it's not him."

I tried to keep calm. Tried not to worry. *Surely not, Lord. Please, don't let it be Mark.*

Thirty minutes had passed. I tried Mark's cell phone a third time. Voice mail picked up immediately.

> *I tried to keep calm. Tried not to worry.* Surely not, Lord. Please, don't let it be Mark.

Moments later, Mark's best friend, PJ, called from the University of Dayton where he was in ROTC. A mutual friend of his and Mark's had seen information about the crash on the internet. That friend immediately called PJ.

"I'm sure this is Mark's unit, Mrs. Lalli!" said PJ.

Since neither of us had any official information, we brainstormed.

"Let me see if I can ask my commander if there is any way he can find anything out," said PJ, as he hung up the phone.

Over the next several hours, more details were released. I read internet updates on the computer. Four confirmed dead. Five confirmed dead. Six of the eleven on board did not survive the crash. But names were being withheld until the first of kin were notified. I breathed a sigh of relief, but I still continued to try Mark's phone a couple more times with the hope that miraculously he might answer.

I tried to be rational. Since I hadn't heard anything, I had no reason to worry. There was no reason to believe Mark or any of the soldiers from his unit were on board. After all, Aviano was an air base. Thousands of airmen were stationed there.

A couple of hours later, our home phone rang. It was someone named Jess. Mark briefly mentioned he'd met a young woman from Australia. He'd asked if she could come home with him over the holidays.

"Mark is alive," she said, voice quavering. "But he's in critical condition. He's in a coma."

> *"Mark is alive," Jess said. "But he's in critical condition. He's in a coma."*

A soldier friend of Mark's took the phone.

"We are really not supposed to call you, Mrs. Lalli. It's against protocol and we could go to jail for this," he whispered. "I have to hang up, but Mark is all right. They'll call you soon. He's alive."

I put my head in my hands and cried. I felt terrified that Mark had been injured in the crash, but grateful that he survived. *My faccia brutto.* Both of my full-blooded Italian parents were first-generation Americans, so I grew up with the language in an Italian neighborhood in New York. I wasn't fluent, but I could read and understand Italian well enough to know what was going on when others were speaking.

I often called Mark *faccia brutto,* a playful Italian term of endearment which literally translated to "ugly face." Not that Mark was ugly—he was just the opposite, with curly brown locks that dangled in ringlets if we did not cut his hair short enough, big brown eyes, and long, thick eyelashes. He was such a beautiful child that strangers often stopped me when he was young.

"What a pretty little girl," they'd remark.

I shook the memory out of my mind. Mark always hated when I told that story.

After school one day when he was in first grade, I called him faccia brutto as I often did.

"Yeah," he retorted. "People tell me I look like my mother."

From that moment on, it was our private joke. He had a wicked sense of humor, even as a child.

Later that afternoon, the official notification came from a US Air Force colonel, the chief flight surgeon. He said Mark was in a coma. He had fractured his skull, had many broken bones, and had numerous other injuries. He began to list them, but it was too much to comprehend. My hands shook.

He apologized for taking so long to call me. "Protocol dictates that we notify the families of the six fallen soldiers first."

My shoulders relaxed. Up until that time, I'd not considered anyone else's pain. I prayed silently in my mind: *Dear God! Please comfort those families who lost loved ones.*

The colonel said I'd soon receive a call from Mark's headquarters in Germany to inform us about travel arrangements. We needed to get on a plane as soon as possible—just in case.

I called our older son, Peter, who was in medical school doing a fellowship with the Cleveland Clinic about forty minutes away, and broke the news to him. My husband was working in Pennsylvania. He jumped in his car for the six-hour drive home.

News about Mark's accident spread like wildfire. Carolyn, my friend from church who had called initially, contacted the parish office at

St. Matthew's Episcopal to put us on the prayer list. The rector showed up at the door moments after I received confirmation about Mark, as did a few other friends. I'm so glad they were there to help me figure out what I should do and what questions I should ask.

PJ had called his mother earlier while he waited for news. She'd just gotten home from her regular morning Mass, but went back to the parish, to pray and give Mark's name to the intercessory prayer team, even though she wasn't sure at the time if Mark was on that helicopter or not.

"Lord, please let him live" was my constant prayer. My only prayer.

In fact, I later learned that within an hour of when I first heard of Mark's accident, he was on five church prayer lists. Within twelve hours of the accident, people from every church in town were praying for him.

Somebody would call their church and say, "We need to put Mark Lalli's name on the prayer list," and the church secretary would say, "Oh yes, it has been on there for a couple of hours now. We are praying for him."

So much of the day was a blur. It was so hard to think straight. There were so many unknowns. "Lord, please let him live" was my constant prayer. My only prayer. I was too afraid to pray anything more than that. I couldn't bear the thought that my son, my baby boy, might not make it. He was only twenty-two—too young to die.

I moved through the rest of the day on autopilot. My body was there, but my mind? I'm not sure where my mind went. Maybe I was in shock. How else could a mother cope with the devastating news that her son was gravely injured and near death?

My own army—my army of friends—sprang into action. Like me, most had traded their full-time careers for family life when they had children. They might have been "just volunteers" over the last two decades, but they knew better than many paid professionals how to get things done.

Someone's daughter-in-law's mother was a travel agent. She found the best flight from Cleveland to Venice and held three seats.

"What do you want me to do?" was the common question everyone asked. When I couldn't answer, they thought for me.

"Let us pack for you."

Someone pulled my green suitcase out of the closet and went to work.

Lunch and dinner somehow arrived in the kitchen. I'm not sure who ordered it, when it arrived, or who paid for it. I didn't feel like eating, but my friends sat with me. They encouraged me to take a few bites to keep my strength up.

Our kitchen phone rang off the wall. I called my brother and Rich's brothers' families to brief them on our situation.

Peter arrived a short time later, and Rich came home later that night. We sat on the couch, held each other, and cried in between phone calls and visits from the army and friends, late into the night.

A Light from Above

I was no longer falling through the air toward the ground and certain death. The horrific sight of terrified faces and ear-piercing sounds of screams and rushing wind from the helicopter was gone.

Ever so gradually, like someone slowly pushing up the lights on a dimmer switch, I aroused into consciousness. Before me was a breathtaking view. More spectacular than anything I'd ever seen in all my travels around the world with the army. Italy, Spain, France—even the Alps didn't compare to the splendor of this place where I was now. In fact, my eyes beheld a sight more beautiful than any postcard photograph I'd ever sent back to my folks at home.

A vast green landscape stretched out in front of me, almost like a huge pasture, but the tall grass was well watered and pristinely cut.

This was the most gorgeous place I'd ever seen.

There were no animals grazing, or even present there, but in the distance I could hear birds happily chirping. The colors of this meadow were vibrant, greens of all shades—dark green, light green, yellow-green. They mixed with brown, amber, and golden hues.

Looking around at this rural place, I was vaguely reminded of the scenery in Pennsylvania and West Virginia that I saw out the back seat car window as Dad drove us to our grandparents' house in New Jersey each summer. Lush, picture-perfect backdrops with trees, rocks, and the big, open sky.

But this was more beautiful. It was the most gorgeous place I'd ever seen.

In the midst of this acreage, a few very tall pine trees, maybe ponderosa pines, dotted the landscape. Their rich colors, like that of the field, glowed with vibrancy. I watched as the tops of their branches swayed ever so slightly in the breeze. But oddly, I didn't feel the wind or see any other evidence of it.

Farther beyond the field was a majestic mountain range. Darker shades of green, tan, and brown didn't dull with the distance, even though the mountainous region had to be many miles away. Amazingly, the outline of the mountains was sharp, crisp, in focus, and not blurred, as something so far away usually was in real life.

The most awesome part of this picturesque place was the deep blue sky. Above me, the azure stratosphere shimmered with brightness, despite the sun not being visible. Instead, I saw fluffy white clouds hanging near the mountains and high in the sky overhead. Like gigantic puffs of cotton candy, their billowy shapes and sizes dotted the windless sky. Their whiteness was purer and more serene than the first Ohio winter snowfall.

I had absolutely no idea where I was, but strangely I didn't care or wonder about it either. Everything was calm, quiet, and pleasant. An overwhelming sense of contentment, peace, and well-being enveloped me. The experience was extremely vivid and real, yet at the same time it felt surreal. I didn't understand what was actually happening or going to happen, but I knew one thing for certain: everything before me existed. This place was not an illusion or dream. It was more beautiful than my imagination could possibly create.

I was sitting on the long, rectangular porch of a reddish-brown log cabin. A few feet in front of me on the edge of a raised, wood-planked porch was a rustic split rail fence. The bench I sat on, too, was made of a split log, maybe four or five feet long. I could feel the roughness of it under my jeans.

I sat on the left side of the bench, but I wasn't there alone. Someone sat beside me, on my right. It was as if we'd been sitting there forever, like He'd been beside me all along.

Next to me, near enough to touch, was an otherworldly object that radiated an intense light—a giant glowing orb. But the orb wasn't so much an object as it was a being. All knowing and intelligent, it exuded an essence of love.

Bigger than me, yet still able to be contained on the bench beside me, the being was oval-shaped, taller and wider than my body. The intense light glowed like embers, but unlike fire, nothing was consumed. It never really moved but brilliantly shone. It was blinding, yet it didn't hurt my eyes.

The color was golden, but unlike any golden color I'd ever seen before. It reminded me of an effervescent twenty-four-karat, pure liquid gold that was mixed with the illumination of the midday sun. A mixture of gold and yellow, or a deep goldish-yellow, almost a deeper amber, like a giant, glowing amber stone.

Even though this orb looked unlike anything I'd ever seen before, I wasn't afraid. In fact it was just the opposite. I felt all-encompassing joy and contentment sitting next to this blazing radiance. Intuitively, I knew that the pulsating aura was a divine presence. I understood it was God. As it says in the book of John, God is light; in him there is no darkness at all. God was this light. And I could feel His unconditional love, peace, and joy flowing through and around my being.

Did I die? Is this heaven?

We sat together in silence, staring out at the pastoral scene in front of the cabin. I'm not sure if we sat there for a minute, an hour, a day, a week, or a month. In this place, time didn't seem to exist. It had no meaning. I felt like I could have been sitting there for ten minutes, but it could have been ten weeks. There was no sense of time.

Finally, I spoke. I turned to the orb. His brightness should have blinded me, but it didn't.

"Hey, you know, this is really nice," I said out loud, as if I were talking to one of my army buddies over a beer at the canteen. I felt conscious and alert, just like I'd felt when I was with the guys at the base—guys I'd known for years and trusted with my life.

"Can I stay here for a while?"

I had no memory of the existence I'd just had, but sitting on this porch felt so pleasant and welcoming that I never wanted to leave.

A loud, strong, yet calming voice answered back. "No, you have to go back. You have work to do."

I'm not sure if I heard Him actually speak out loud or if the sound of His voice resonated through my mind, but

> *I had no memory of the existence I'd just had, but sitting here felt so pleasant and welcoming that I never wanted to leave.*

either way, I felt disappointed. It wasn't the answer I was looking for. All I wanted was to stay in this spot forever—for eternity.

Even though I felt one hundred percent alive and in my body, like I was actually there on the porch and having a conversation in first person, I also felt like I was watching the two of us from a third-person perspective, like what you see on a TV show or movie when the cameras film different points of view. Even while I was talking to God, in the perspective of my point of view, I simultaneously saw a panoramic sort of long shot of the entire setting—the cabin, the porch, and the two of us. Me with a short-sleeved shirt on, sitting on a bench with a glowing orb and the landscape that surrounded us.

I was sitting there, tuned in to this spiritual being who told me to go back against my will, yet I wasn't angry. Instead, I had a great sense of calm.

Moments or months later—I'm not sure which, since time had no meaning—God spoke again. I had an awareness that His arm was around my shoulder, but I couldn't see an outstretched arm or anything outside the incandescent ball of light. I also couldn't feel the weight of the arm resting on my shoulders, but I had a strong sense that God had His arm around me.

"You have been in a bad way, but you can do better," He said. "You've got to get better. You've got to move forward and move on."

> *Even though the Lord called me out and corrected me, I didn't feel chastised. His words held no judgment or condemnation.*

Immediately, I knew what He was talking about. I remembered my prayer from two years earlier, the promise I made to God when I first got to Iraq and Kuwait: "If you can see me through this year, I will be better. I will do good. I will help people. I will live for someone other than myself."

I had made it through that year in Iraq. I got through it with no physical damage, but my way of living never changed. In other words, I didn't hold up my side of the bargain. I didn't keep my word to God.

Even though the Lord called me out and corrected me, I didn't feel chastised. His tone was very matter-of-fact, like He was giving me advice the way my father used to. His words held no judgment or condemnation.

"You know, you made a promise that you would do this, but you are not doing it. You're doing the opposite. You need to go back. You need to do something good with your life. You need to do something good for others. You made a promise before; now you need to live up to that promise."

There was not a doubt in my mind that this spiritual being was God. He knew things about me, my secret prayer that no one else could have known.

Feeling as if I'd let down the Creator of the universe, I was disappointed in myself too. Although his tone wasn't angry, I had a sense that He was disappointed in me. Like my father would say to me when I was growing up: "Son, I'm disappointed with you. I'm not mad, but I'm disappointed."

Deep down, I knew I hadn't been my best self. I wasn't surprised that God was disappointed in me too. I understood I'd let Him down, but instead of feeling judged, I felt reassured. Like hearing an inspirational children's message from Father Alan, I felt encouraged to try harder. I wanted to make amends. Do the right thing. Be a better person.

A calm, comfortable confidence covered me. *You know what? I will do better!* I felt fully known and fully loved with an unconditional paternal love. *I'll be better to my family, my friends, and my community. I will do more good.*

The two of us sat there a moment longer in this celestial realm. Eventually, the rural scene and my time with God on the porch of the log cabin faded out much like the way it started. The last thing I felt was the sense that He still had His arm around my shoulder. I knew what I had to do. I had to keep my promise. Everything slowly faded to black.

A Mother's Plea: Dear God, Please

Rich, Peter, and I flew overnight and arrived in Venice early Friday morning. An American army representative dressed in camouflage fatigues and a priest wearing a black suit and clerical collar were easy to spot when we got to baggage claim. Beside them was a young blonde woman—Jess, Mark's girlfriend.

"Well, this cannot be good if you are here waiting for us, Father," I said.

Father Kaim met my gaze. He pursed his lips tightly as he slowly looked at each of our faces.

"Mark is fighting for his life," he said solemnly. "We're going to go straight to the hospital."

On the car ride over, we learned that Mark was the most seriously injured of the five survivors. The air force captain on one side of him and the pilot, who was sitting on the other side, in front of him, were both killed on impact. The second army pilot died Thursday on his way to the hospital.

"You know, Mark was not even supposed to be on that flight," said Jess, a quaver in her voice. "It was a last-minute change. They weren't in Mark's helicopter that day."

At the Ospedale Di Treviso, a regional teaching hospital, we walked to the neurology ICU waiting area. Unlike ICUs in American hospitals, this floor was always on lockdown.

Father Kaim knocked on the door and spoke in Italian to the medical person inside. Moments later, a doctor appeared.

"I want to prepare you. Mark's in pretty bad shape," he said through a translator. "He's gravely injured and on life support. I can only let you see him for a few minutes."

I tried to close out his words. I didn't want to understand what he was saying. All I wanted was to see my son. My mother's heart was breaking.

The three of us, along with Jess and Father Kaim, slipped sterile yellow gowns over our clothes. We put bonnets on our heads and booties on our shoes as we walked through the large area that was partitioned off with curtains to form rooms.

The hooks screeched eerily along the metal rod as the doctor pulled back the drape to Mark's room. We stepped inside the tiny cubicle. What I saw made my knees go weak. I fought hard to keep my composure.

My son's lifeless body looked frail and small beneath the stark white sheet, yet every part of his flesh that was exposed was extremely swollen. Among the many wires and tubes that poked out from his flesh were three drainage tubes in his chest, electrodes attached to his temples, a shunt in his head just above his forehead, and an IV in his hand for fluids, nourishment, and medication. His blood pressure was being

Looking at my son's motionless body as I stood helplessly by was the worst single moment of my life.

monitored at his biceps. A wire snaked under his hospital gown to monitor his heartbeat. He had a ventilator down his throat to breathe for him, since both of his lungs were collapsed. A catheter and bag were attached to the side of the bed. His eyes were bruised, cheeks scratched. His back, pelvis, and leg were broken. He had at least thirty broken bones in all.

Dear God, no! Looking at my son's motionless body as I stood helplessly by in that foreign ICU hospital was the worst single moment of my life, without a doubt.

The doctor said that Mark was in a drug-induced coma to keep him sedated due to his intense level of pain. Even when a person is in a coma, he can still feel excruciating pain. And the pain from Mark's injuries would be unbearable without heavy-duty narcotics.

"Would you like me to give him last rites?" whispered Father Kaim.

I nodded my head as I blinked back tears.

Father Kaim walked close to Mark's bed. He stretched out his hand, and made the sign of the cross. He began to say the series of prayers.

"Through this holy anointing may the Lord in his love and mercy help you with the grace of the Holy Spirit. May the Lord who frees you from sin save you and raise you up."

He took a small bottle of oil out of his pocket and dabbed it on his finger. He gently pressed his fingertips against Mark's forehead, just above his eyebrows.

Father Kaim continued with the twenty-third psalm and said another prayer.

Mark lay quiet and still, the hum of medical equipment and the chug of the ventilator breathing for him the only sounds that competed with Father's voice.

He concluded with St. Michael the Archangel's prayer.

"I've seen lots of tattoos in the military, but this is the first time I've seen St. Michael that size. It takes up his whole upper arm."

I nodded.

"That's why I decided to include St. Michael's prayer. It must be special to him," said the priest. He encouraged us to come close to the bed and talk to Mark.

"Mark," I said, trying to keep my voice from shaking. "It's Mom. Dad, Peter, and Jess are here too."

Rich reached out his hand and rubbed Mark's forearm. I watched tears stream down Rich's face.

The nurse advised us to talk to Mark as if he were awake. We told him about the flight over, how we knew he was going to get better, and that everyone back home was praying for him. I tried to keep it light-hearted to break the tension.

"You have to get well so you can show us around Europe, faccia brutto."

My words hung in the air. There was no response.

Since Peter was studying to be an immunologist, he knew what kinds of questions we needed to ask.

"Where does Mark score on the Glasgow Scale?" Peter turned to the translator, who asked the nurse.

The nurse hesitated. "*Tre.*"

Peter's expression fell. Tears pooled in the corners of his eyes. He covered his face with his hands and walked beyond the curtain.

The look on the nurse's face didn't need translation. I saw that my son's survival might not be a possibility.

The nurse ushered all of us out. The translator relayed her words that visiting hours were at 3:30 in the afternoon. We could come back tomorrow, if Mark made it through the night. But the look on her face didn't need translation. I saw in her eyes that my son's survival might not be a possibility.

The army had arranged for us to stay in transitional living quarters, an apartment. On our way there, I asked Peter about his question to the nurse.

"What does it mean?"

Peter explained that a score of three on the Glasgow Scale was totally unresponsive. It was the lowest a patient could score out of fifteen points for a hopeful recovery from a coma.

"That's pretty bad, isn't it?" I said.

Peter paused and sniffed back tears. "It's the worst you could be without being dead."

The driver dropped Jess off. The three of us cried and prayed the rest of the evening.

At the hospital the next afternoon, we waited with a roomful of other families. The doctors appeared about 3:30 and called each patient's family for a brief consultation. They'd discuss what happened with the patient in the past twenty-four hours. Once every family had been updated, we all scrubbed up and put on sterile gowns to spend half an hour with our loved one. But I learned that, very often, they relaxed the rules and allowed families to stay a bit longer.

The Aviano Air Base Family Readiness Group (FRG) cooked meals for us and supplied all our needs. We had free rein on the base. Two of Mark's friends were assigned as our drivers to take us to and from the hospital.

On the second day, on our way to see Mark, I read the Italian street signs. It seemed the driver was not taking us on the most direct route. My Italian was limited, but I could still read the sign for the exit to the hospital as we drove past it.

The following day, I heard our military representative exclaim in Italian to the driver.

"Hey! We're not supposed to go this way because of the crash site. Remember to take them the other route on the way back."

I fixed my eyes out the windows. In the distance, near an open clearing by the river, was a huge heap of mangled metal—the wreckage of Mark's downed Black Hawk. My heart sank.

Days later, after the investigation concluded, the wreckage was gone and we took the direct route.

That Sunday, we met the air force doctor liaison who had been assigned to Mark's case. She confided that they thought he wouldn't have made it through the night when he was brought in on Thursday.

The original report that was written when Mark was admitted stated that if he lived, he would probably not awaken from the coma.

"When I woke up Friday morning, I was in a panic because no one alerted me," she said. "We expected he would code overnight, but there were no messages on my phone. I called the lab and they confirmed Mark was still very critical, but holding his own."

She explained that Mark was almost stable enough to do a CT scan of his head and all the broken bones including his scapula, ribs, pelvis, back, and leg.

I told her many people were praying for him.

"Well, that's what he needs," she said candidly. Her dark eyes shone with compassion.

She explained that the original report that was written when Mark was admitted the day of the accident stated that if he lived, he would probably not awaken from the coma. It was the admitting physician's opinion that Mark would remain in a vegetative state.

"I pray that's an incorrect prognosis," she whispered. "Keep your faith."

Mark's condition remained touch and go for the next few days. I had no idea how long we would be in Europe, but I knew one thing—Mark wouldn't be released any time soon.

Peter flew back to the States the following Wednesday to take care of things for us there. The army drove us to the Venice airport, which was about an hour away. Jess came with us to say goodbye to Peter. Afterward, she had a suggestion.

"We need to go into St. Mark's Basilica and light candles," she said. "That's what Mark does every time we come to Venice."

Rich and I nodded.

I poured out my heart, begging for God's mercy, Mark's healing, and a miracle.

Immediately after stepping inside the dark eleventh-century cathedral, calmness descended on us. I bowed and genuflected before walking farther into the cavernous sanctuary. We found a station toward the back of the church, made a donation, and lit candles. We knelt there on a bench at the candle station, and bowed our heads in prayer. I poured out my heart, begging for God's mercy, Mark's healing, and a miracle. *Dear God, please. Let him live.*

We ordered something to eat at a sidewalk café close to the Piazza San Marco square. It was a lovely setting, but I had no appetite for the delicious soup. I couldn't help but wonder how different I would feel if Mark were here with us—if we'd flown over to sightsee with him, instead of standing by his ICU bed, watching him fight for his life.

We took the train back to Treviso. On the bumpy ride through the Italian countryside, Rich got a text from Mark's doctor at the hospital: "Things are looking up. I'll meet you at the hospital."

As Rich read me the text, I sighed with relief. Mark still had a long way to go. Doctors were unsure how much progress he was capable of, but I knew someone who did. *Thank You, God. You heard our prayers.*

Every day I waited for confirmation that Mark could hear us, that his mind was still alive inside his broken body. Everything we did and said was with the goal of getting him to respond.

Jess's mother convinced her to return to Sydney the following Sunday, about ten days after the crash. I told her she could come to the States to see Mark once he was home.

A Mother's Journey: Days Melted into Weeks

Mark's progress was slow. Coming out of a coma wasn't anything like the way movies or television dramas portrayed it. Mark's eyes were often open, but that didn't really mean anything. He didn't always respond to touch. The doctor warned us that Mark's recuperation would be a long, arduous process. They had no idea what he would be capable of—or if he would even be able to wake up from the coma.

In order to determine the true extent of the brain injuries and how Mark's brain was healing would require an MRI. But that was not possible because of the ventilator, all the tubes in his chest, and the tubes in his brain.

He had broken his back, eight vertebrae, pelvis, and ribs. The doctor thought Mark's leg was broken and had stabilized it with a brace since he was too weak for surgery. Mark's broken bones were beginning to heal naturally and much of the swelling had gone down. In addition, the contusions in his brain and lungs had gotten smaller. But two steps forward, one step back. He developed pneumonia in one lung and a round of antibiotics was added to his IV.

It would take another week or two for the inflammation in his brain to go down and the bruises in his lungs to heal. No one expected him to have made it this far, and every day Rich and I continued to pray for a miracle.

The next week, the swelling on his brain had decreased enough for the shunt in his head to be removed. Doctors began to reduce the amount of sedation that kept him in the coma. Mark's condition remained grave, but he slowly, steadily improved. He occasionally opened his eyes, but I could tell he wasn't seeing us. I prayed this was just a transition from being in a coma—that it wouldn't be a permanent state. Doctors and nurses warned it was a long process.

> *I was used to fixing everything. I yearned for a way to make it all better.*

It was extremely frustrating—the waiting, not seeing results. As a mother, I was used to fixing everything. I yearned for a way to make it all better. The days of kissing a scraped elbow and sending Mark back outside to play were a distant memory from a life far away.

A physician suggested we bring music that Mark liked, so his buddies helped us download songs from his computer and make a couple of CDs. Nurses put earphones in his ears and turned on a portable CD player each morning.

Father Kaim accompanied us to the hospital a couple of times. A few of Mark's friends visited him too. Each afternoon, we talked to Mark about where we were staying, friends of his that we'd met, and how we cleaned out his apartment to ready his things to be shipped home.

"Well, my goodness!" I said, in an exaggerated tone. "I know that you are not the neatest person, Mark, but it's a good thing we were the ones who cleaned out your apartment. If the army would have seen the way things were strung around your place, they would have dispatched the MPs to find whoever had broken in there and made such a mess."

But Mark showed no reaction.

By the third week we noticed movement in his shoulders and hands. He still had a fever and was battling pneumonia, but the nurse was able to set the ventilator to assist his breathing just when he needed help. One afternoon when Mark heard Rich's voice, he opened his eyes. Even though they were not focused, we took it as a good sign.

The doctors still couldn't give us a prognosis, but they were astounded at Mark's progress. He was doing better than any of them initially predicted. By the end of that third week, he came off the respirator completely. All of his stitches were removed, and the tubes in his chest had come out.

During the fourth week in the hospital, Mark was still feverish with pneumonia and had contracted a hospital infection called C. diff. But his eyes often fluttered when he heard our voices. We asked him questions and encouraged him to talk. He made some grunts.

The Italian doctors felt that Mark would be stable enough to fly to Walter Reed Army Medical Center in the States and continue his recovery there; however, the army doctor at the Vicenza army base was not as optimistic. He predicted Mark would remain in a vegetative state and needed to be in a long-term care facility. We prayed and asked everyone back home to pray that Mark proved him wrong.

We never heard what caused the crash, but one of the airmen who survived told the investigators that had it not been for Mark's preflight safety instruction, he wouldn't have made it. Another survivor wrote us a note and said the same thing. That gave us a reason to be proud in the midst of the tragedy. And to think I used to tease him about being a glorified stewardess.

Four weeks after Mark arrived at the Italian hospital, doctors felt he was stable enough to be transferred in order to be flown to the United States. The army liaison suggested we go home and regroup for a week before joining Mark at Walter Reed in Washington, DC, to continue his recovery. Rich and I reluctantly flew home.

Mark was transferred to a hospital that was closer to the base for a few days in order to prepare him for the move to Landstuhl, Germany; from there, he would fly on a hospital plane to Walter Reed, where all the head and brain trauma cases were seen.

While Mark was at Landstuhl for approximately a week, Master Sergeant (MSG) Semco was our family contact. He went in to see Mark a couple times a day. He dutifully called with updates while we waited in Ohio for Mark to arrive in the United States.

The day before Mark was to fly to the States, MSG Semco called with good news.

"I asked Mark if he had a brother named Peter. He answered 'yes.' I asked him if he was from Ohio. Mark again answered 'yes.' Then I asked if he liked to rock climb. This time Mark said 'yes' in a quieter voice," said MSG Semco, his tone happy. "I said in a louder voice: 'Sgt. Lalli, I can't hear you. What did you say?' And Mark strongly answered, 'yes.' This is a very good sign, Mrs. Lalli."

I couldn't contain my excitement. Rich and I jumped up and down, laughing and crying with joy. The liaison told us that Mark was on the manifest to fly out the next day, but would not arrive at Andrews Air Force Base until later that evening. It had been nearly a week since we had seen him. I couldn't wait to be with him again. I was especially excited to see how much progress he'd made.

Days later, Rich and I drove to Walter Reed. Mark had arrived just after dinner a couple hours earlier. The nurse was getting him prepped for scans and X-rays in the ICU step-down unit. We stood in the doorway.

"Hello, Mark. It's Mom. Dad and I are here. Can you say, 'Hi, Mom'?" I waited hopefully.

Rich and I chatted away, ignoring the fact that the conversation was mostly one sided.

"Hi, Mom," Mark repeated in a low, monotone voice.

We walked to his bedside. A nurse was trying to put an IV in his arm. It took her several pokes to get it.

"Ow, crap!" hollered Mark.

The three of us laughed.

"I bet that hurts," I said.

"Yes," replied Mark.

Like always, Rich and I chatted away, ignoring the fact that the conversation was mostly one sided. After the nurse finished with the IV, I sat in the chair next to the bed. Rich sat beside me on the arm of the recliner.

We talked about our drive into Washington and our hotel.

"Remember when we took a vacation to the Capitol when you were a kid?" Rich asked.

Mark didn't answer. We figured he must be tired. We mentioned things that were happening in Ohio—how a couple of his high school buddies had stopped by our house while they were home from college for the holidays. We told him what was going on in our town and at church.

"So many people have been praying for you," I said, patting his hand.

"I know," Mark said quietly. "I heard them."

Rich and I exchanged looks.

"We sure have missed you," I said, squeezing his hand. "It is so good to see you again, faccia brutto."

It took a few seconds, but Mark lifted his gaze. He slightly turned his head toward my face.

"I look like my mother," he said slowly. He gently squeezed my hand.

A huge smile spread across my face. Rich and I burst out laughing.

"Oh, thank God!" said Rich. "He's back!"

After a month at Walter Reed, Mark was transferred to a polytrauma rehab center for intensive rehabilitation.

Alive, but Severely Wounded

That spring, I slowly began to rouse from my coma. I'd been at James A. Haley Veterans' Hospital in Tampa, Florida, for about three months. I still wore a back brace and braces on my leg and arm to hold my bones in place while they continued to heal naturally. Additionally, I suffered from a traumatic brain injury (TBI), partial paralysis, post-traumatic stress disorder (PTSD), and depression.

At the polytrauma rehabilitation center, physical therapists, occupational therapists, and speech therapists came to my room to work with me daily. Mom moved to Tampa so she could be with me. Dad was still working in Cleveland, but he flew out as frequently as he could.

Besides working my physical muscles to gain the strength to sit, stand, and move again, I had to practice simple daily tasks like feeding myself, getting dressed, and brushing my teeth. The accident had erased many memories. My speech therapist worked to help me regain my cognitive functions and increase my attention span. He had me do memory exercises, since my short-term memory was virtually nonexistent.

I had some good days and many not-so-good ones. The pain was intense. I had difficulty sleeping and often felt irritated and agitated. Sometimes, I'd get so keyed up that I couldn't relax or calm myself down. I'd fidget, sweat, and move restlessly, unable to get comfortable. I used to be a calm, copacetic guy, so this newfound anxiety troubled me.

> *The neurologist said my recovering brain was rewiring itself. He explained that my brain would go through ups and downs before it could regulate itself.*

The neurologist said my feelings were appropriate as my recovering brain was rewiring itself. He explained that my brain would go through phases of ups and downs before it could regulate itself.

"You have progressed so quickly over these past few months," he assured me.

But to me, I progressed at a snail's pace. I tried to keep positive—think of all the things I could do. But the list of what I couldn't do taunted me.

I was bed bound for the first few months. I was partially paralyzed due to the TBI and my shattered pelvis, so it was tough to control my right leg. Walking proved extremely difficult, so I learned to use a wheelchair.

I had no memory of the crash, the three hospitals I was in before I came to Tampa, or the months I lay in a coma. But I did have one very vivid memory. I'm not sure exactly when the experience had happened—maybe right after the crash, or a while later. I'm also not sure how long it lasted, maybe an hour, or days, or months. But this scene—no, more like a conversation—floated through my mind.

As I lay on my back recovering, piece by piece, the memory stirred. Usually it happened when I relaxed, when I let my mind travel wherever it wanted instead of the usual requirement of pushing hard to make my brain think.

I was in a pastoral setting, sitting on a rustic bench. A feeling of comfort and calm enveloped me as I drank in the beauty before me. Peaceful meadows with trees. Mountains in the background. A glowing orb sat by my side.

> *The experience lingered in the shadows of my mind like the happy memories I had of playing with Grandpa Nick.*

The memory felt like it had been with me forever, but I'm sure I didn't know about it before the crash. Still, it wasn't a dream. I knew it wasn't a dream. In dreams things often are discombobulated and don't make sense. In that place, everything made sense. It was peaceful.

The experience lingered in the shadows of my mind like the happy memories I had of playing with Grandpa Nick. Even though he'd passed on more than a decade ago, I still felt him near. That's how it was with this experience.

I often asked my parents for details about the crash and what happened to the other crew members I flew with that day, but they changed the subject. I asked the psychiatrist and counselors, too, but they wouldn't say either. In group therapy, I talked about my feelings—about the accident, my wounds, and the recovery process. But my hope for a life that held meaning with a military career dwindled.

One kind physical therapist's aide tried to encourage me, saying I had a hope and a future. The phrase was so familiar, I knew she was referencing the verse in Jeremiah 29:11. Pointing me back to God: "'For I know the plans I have for you,' declares the LORD, 'plans to prosper you and not to harm you, plans to give you a hope and a future.'"

But I was too exhausted to think deeply. Maybe all my energy was taken up with healing my broken mind and body. I tried to pray, but God felt far away. I couldn't help but consider the irony that I'd risked my life in a combat zone, but it was on a routine assignment in Europe that I became critically injured. As much as I wanted to know what happened to the other soldiers that day, I felt I must have been one of the lucky ones—one of the protected ones who had received a second chance at life. Why wouldn't anyone give me the accident details I craved?

One afternoon, I lay in my bed, agitated and frustrated with my extremely slow recovery pace. Physically, I was always sore and in so much pain. Mentally, my mind and memory were still foggy. Recovering was hard work, but with my many injuries I wondered if it would even be worth it. What kind of life could a guy like me expect?

Knock. Knock. Knock.

Before I could holler "Come in," the door handle turned. A stranger peeked in. He had a dark, closely cropped military haircut, and he wore a black polo shirt and a pair of shorts with a backpack slung over his shoulder. He looked to be about a decade older than me. Maybe thirtyish.

"Hi, I'm Jonathan," he said with a smile.

He walked to my bedside with a slight limp.

"Here, I brought you a milkshake." He held out a fast-food cup.

As he came closer to my bed, I noticed he was wearing a prosthetic. He caught me looking at the metal pole that served as his lower leg.

"Roadside bomb—IED [improvised explosive device] in Iraq, 2003," he said. "My leg was amputated just below my knee."

I took a long sip of the creamy milkshake as I listened.

"I can't run, but I can swim, kayak, hike, bike, and go hunting. I've even been deep-sea fishing," he said. "Army retired me a few years ago, but thanks to the Wounded Warrior Project, I live an active, productive life."

Jonathan put the backpack on the bed. It contained a few sundries and brochures about the services WWP provided. We talked a few minutes more. I couldn't help but admire him.

"When I got injured, I thought my life was over," he said sincerely. "But now I have a great job encouraging soldiers like you. And the best thing? My wife and I are expecting a baby!"

He smiled broadly and told me he'd visit again. My memory was so bad, but I was glad I remembered one thing before he left.

"Thanks for the milkshake," I called, as he closed my door.

Jonathan had inspired me. If he could do all that with one leg gone, what was my excuse? Even though my recovery was hard and I knew it was bound to get harder, it would be worth it. I determined to succeed.

My Biggest Battle

Six months after the crash, I figured out that everyone was hiding the details about the helicopter accident from me. I'd questioned medical personnel, my parents, even Jess when she flew to the States to visit me for a few months while I recuperated here. No one would give me a straight answer. I wanted to know what happened. I had the right to know the truth. That's when I had an idea.

During my occupational therapy sessions over the past couple weeks, we'd practiced typing on the keyboard. I sent emails and accessed social media accounts from a computer. I'd even typed an entry on my mom's blog. That's when it hit me. If I could send an email, I could access the internet. If I could access the internet, I could find out what had happened.

> No one had determined the cause of the crash. But I was the senior crew chief. Had I missed something?

Instead of resting in my bed after lunch like I usually did, I rolled my wheelchair down to the computer lab. I logged on and searched: Aviano helicopter crash. A link from a *Stars and Stripes* article came up with the headline: "Six Black Hawk Crash Victims Identified."

My heart felt like it was going to beat out of my chest as I clicked on the link. I read the news story. Six of the eleven on board had died. Out of the four in my company on board, two had perished. Two of my friends. Both the pilots, Captain Skoglund and CW2 Alvarez, were gone.

I put my head on the desk and cried.

The investigation was ongoing, and no one had determined the cause of the crash. But I was the senior crew chief that day. *Had I missed* something? *Was there something I could have done to prevent this? Something I failed to do?* I couldn't help but feel racked with guilt.

I wheeled my chair down to talk to the psychologist. We discussed it in therapy group later that week. I even talked to Father Alan. They all said the same thing—I had survivor's guilt.

There was nothing that could have been done. Nothing that I could have done differently. I felt guilty because I was alive while my fellow soldiers died. It was a false sense of guilt, even if it didn't feel that way.

One afternoon, Jonathan, the Wounded Warrior Project representative, stopped by my room. I told him that I found out about the accident. I confided my guilt.

> *He told me that November 8, 2007, was my Alive Day and that it was my duty to honor those who didn't survive by living my best day each day for them.*

He was quiet for a moment, then sat down on the edge of my bed.

"November 8, 2007, changed your life forever," he whispered.

He told me that I had a choice. I could make myself crazy trying to remember the events of the crash. I could let that tragedy live and grow in my mind by wrongly assuming there was something I could have done to change the outcome. He assured me there was nothing that I could have possibly done to prevent the hard landing.

"You know what November 8, 2007, really is?" he asked.

I shrugged my shoulders, but continued to listen intently.

"It's your Alive Day," Jonathan said, nodding his head. "You survived. It's now your duty to remember and honor those who didn't by living your best day each day for them."

"Yes, sir," I answered. "That will be my mission."

From then on, I tried not to dwell on what I couldn't control. I had a lot of other things to worry about as far as my recovery, things that I could actually try to do something about. The process of rehabilitation was physically demanding and emotionally exhausting.

But the bright spot was Jess. She'd gotten a six-month visa to visit me in Florida. She stayed with Mom at the Fisher House, a nonprofit, long-term, family housing facility for relatives of patients at the veterans' hospital.

Jess went to many therapy appointments with me. I had to admit, having her here made me try harder. One afternoon after physical therapy to strengthen my legs, I collapsed into my bed. Jess had faithfully come to the hospital each day to encourage me for the past couple months. I was so grateful to her.

As I sat back on my bed, the words tumbled out of my mouth. "I want to marry you."

Jess sat in the chair next to my bed. She smiled quietly. "I want you to walk."

I spent two years in extensive rehabilitation at James A. Haley Veterans' Hospital in Tampa, Florida. I was promoted to staff sergeant while I was in rehab, but on July 30, 2010, the army retired me because of my injuries. It was understandable, but I was disappointed. My career had come to an end. I was only twenty-four.

Mom, Jess, and I moved into a transitional apartment close to the VA hospital. I continued with outpatient rehabilitation, slowly getting stronger and more independent each day. Jess continued to push me to walk. It was very important to her, but the doctors didn't know if I would ever be able to walk independently again.

By August, her visa ran out and she flew back to Australia. I had an international cellular plan so we could talk on the phone daily. Being on opposite sides of the planet gave me the opportunity to reflect. We'd barely known each other when she came to Italy—maybe a month. Then I went to Romania for three months. I had been back for just two weeks when the accident happened. Yes, she had visited me in the States over the past two and a half years, but we still didn't know each other that well.

> *I could tell Jess focused on what I'd lost, instead of seeing what I had gained. She wasn't the person I needed to travel with me anymore.*

Don't get me wrong. I asked her to marry me, but deep down I wondered if I did it out of love or out of security because I wanted to keep her around. The miles that separated us were not the only distance between us. Emotionally, we weren't close. Actually, we'd never been close. We were just two twenty-one-year-old kids who met in a bar for some fun three years ago, but misfortune had kept us together. We didn't share the same goals or values.

After my injury, Jess treated me differently. I'd made so many strides—I virtually came back from the dead, but she talked down to me. Once she realized the extent of my injuries—that I was permanently disabled and confined to a wheelchair—she treated me with disrespect. Like I was "less than" because of my injuries.

I could tell she focused on what I'd lost, instead of seeing what I had gained. Yes, I had come a long way, but I still had miles to go. And Jess wasn't the person I needed to travel with me anymore. In fact, that might have been what bonded us in the first place—she was gallivanting around Europe, living life free and easy. I loved seeing the sights too—ready to grab any adventure, living life by the seat of my pants. I shook my head. Those days were behind me now.

Although I was afraid of being alone, I knew our relationship wasn't right for either of us. I had to end it. I called and said it was over.

That year was difficult. I relied on Mom for a lot until I was ready to get a car with hand controls and learn to drive again. My life was still all about recovering. I tried to be grateful every day I was alive, not just for myself, but for those who didn't make it that day. For Captain Skoglund and CW2 Alvarez. I knew I couldn't give up. I needed to live my best life to honor their memory.

I slid into depression. *Damaged goods.* That's how I felt. There'd be no happily ever after for me. I survived the crash, but gone was the active, adventuresome, risk-taking G.I. Joe who traveled the world, played ice hockey, kayaked, and rock-climbed. I sat in front of the TV and rarely left home. I survived the crash, but what good was this life? Suicidal thoughts lurked in the back of my mind. They taunted me. *You could do it. You know, you could end it all.*

The only thing stopping me was my faith—I'd been taught it was a sin to take one's life. I tried to feel grateful. Tried to praise God for saving me, but my recovery and life was hard.

When I wasn't doing therapy, I sat in front of the TV most of the time. I stayed inside and rarely went out of my house. I became a shut-in.

What Now?

Dad retired in 2012. He and Mom moved to Tampa and bought a house near me. One day, Mom came over with a familiar-looking book.

"Do you remember this?" she asked.

I slowly turned the pages of the scrapbook. Grandpa Nick's scrapbook. Mom suggested we pick a few items to frame or make a shadow box. Of course, the Santa Fe newspaper when the war ended was something I framed and hung on my wall.

One afternoon, Mom was over at my place watching Netflix with me. We'd started a series called *Longmire,* a six-season Western crime drama about a sheriff named Longmire.

All of a sudden, a rustic log cabin with a big front porch and a pastoral meadow flashed on the screen. I hit pause.

"I've been there," I said to Mom. "This place. I went there."

Mom looked at me curiously.

I told her about the experience I had after the crash.

"Do you think it was a dream you're remembering?"

> *I told Mom about the experience I had after the crash. "It was real. Something happened."*

"Definitely not." I shook my head. "It was real. Something happened. I went to this place."

Then I told her about the conversation on the porch.

"A giant glowing orb sat next to me. I should have been afraid, but I wasn't. I felt an overwhelming calm and love. I told the being that I wanted to stay, but He told me I had to go back," I said. "I knew He was telling me to go back to earth."

Mom nodded.

"I've heard about these sorts of experiences," she said. "They're called near-death experiences, and you were nearly dead, Mark."

We sat in silence for a while.

"Maybe the glowing orb was one of your grandfathers who passed on."

I nodded. "Maybe."

We went back to the Netflix show, but my NDE churned in my mind. The cabin and front porch looked exactly like the place I visited, but the TV show originally premiered on A&E in 2010, two years earlier. The crash was in 2007. *How could that be?*

I failed to tell Mom about the whole conversation. That I made a promise to God that I had not kept. That the orb knew about the promise and urged me to keep my bargain.

I always had the belief that heaven was a reward for following God and for doing the right thing, that when you do that, then you are rewarded by going back to the place, a point in time in your life when you were the most happy. Seeing the cabin and remembering my NDE made me think. I hadn't lived my best yet.

I promised God that I would do good. That I would be a good person and move forward and help others by volunteering in the community.

Mom was wrong. No, that glowing orb wasn't Grandpa Nick or Grandpa Pete. There is only one thing that an all-knowing orb could be. It was God. I knew beyond a shadow of a doubt.

And I also knew I had more work to do. I had to keep moving forward, not only for my brothers who could not move forward anymore, but for God. I had a promise to keep. I didn't want to let Him down again. I needed to be all I could be. I needed to start living my best life, even if that meant I was going to be doing it from the seat of a wheelchair.

Cleveland Cowboy

That October, the WWP invited me to a barbeque at Quantum Leap Farm, an organization that offered a rehabilitative riding program. Horse therapy seemed like fun, but the farm's founder, Edie Dopking, explained that therapeutic riding would help me recapture my balance by working my central core while I was on the back of a horse. I'd never been around horses, but nervously gave it a try.

The next week, apprehension mixed with excitement as I rolled my wheelchair close to the paddock. I was matched with a chestnut appaloosa quarter cross named Sonic. We hit it off immediately. We had a special mojo, and I claimed him as my therapy horse. By the way he greeted me when I came to the farm, I had a feeling he claimed me too.

> *I exhaled my expectations and negative feelings in order to receive the "more" that God had told me about in my NDE.*

At the farm every other week, I rolled my wheelchair to the overhead device that lifted me up, lowered me down, and guided my body onto the saddle. I began each ride the same way—I'd drop the reins, stretch my feet beyond the stirrups, close my eyes, raise my arms skyward into a wide V, and pray.

I imagined myself as one with the horse as I balanced on his back. I inhaled the musty scents of hay and leather. I exhaled my expectations and negative feelings in an attempt to drop the reins of the life I planned in order to receive the "more" that God had told me about in my NDE.

Concentrating on my surroundings, I balanced my body and centered my mind to trust Sonic before we proceeded in tandem through the arena. Rhythmically moving with Sonic's gait strengthened my muscles—even the muscles that I'd lost control of because of the crash.

Therapeutic riding wasn't just a series of physical exercises. There were challenges that focused on mental and emotional health too. At E.A.S.E. allowed for equine-assisted self-exploration. In one exercise, a set of hula hoops was placed on the ground. I had to navigate Sonic through this pseudo minefield while on his back or leading him. The lesson was to get in front of what I could control and walk around that which I couldn't.

Each time I worked with Sonic brought a euphoric rush of joy—joy that I hadn't felt since flying. Driving home from the farm one evening, a thought popped into my mind. *I could really use some direction, God. You put me back here for a reason. It's been more than five years since we talked on the porch. You said You had more for me. Help me find it.*

I signed up for a photography class at the community college. When Edie saw the Canon camera slung around my neck, she asked me to think about volunteering at the ranch. They really needed someone to take photos for the website and social media posts. Of course, I said I would.

New Year's Eve 2012, I was sitting alone in my living room watching TV, when I got a text from PJ's dad. He wanted to wish me a happy new year.

"I have a feeling that thirteen will be our lucky number," he texted.

I had to laugh. "I sure hope so," I texted him back. "I could use some luck!"

Later that evening, as I watched the ball drop on Times Square, I didn't make any resolutions. Instead, I prayed.

God, I need more than luck in 2013. Please send me an angel—someone special who I can share my life with.

I turned off the television, thanked the Lord for another Alive Day, and went to bed.

A New Kind of Service

My wheelchair rolled across the wooden planks of the pergola-shaded deck that Saturday in February 2013. Sonic pricked up his ears when he heard the chug of my wheels. He whipped his head around and sauntered toward the gate.

But I wasn't there to ride this February morning. It was my first day as a volunteer. Edie said the nonprofit organization needed a photographer and I needed something to do—a purpose so I could continue to climb out of the dark place I'd been stuck in since my debilitating accident five years earlier.

After all I'd been through, I held little hope for my future. What "more" could a guy in my situation expect?

Now twenty-seven, I wanted to become my best self, serving my fellow man and God by living a good life. I wanted to claim the "more" God had for me when He sent me back from that rustic log-cabin porch on that heavenly countryside. But after all I'd been through, I held little hope for my future. What "more" could a guy in my situation expect?

Sonic lifted his head over the fence. I pushed up from my chair and leaned against the wooden rail for support as I wrapped my arms around his sleek neck.

"Morning, boy." I rested my forehead on his long nose.

"Hi, Mark!" Edie called as she walked across the patio. "I want you to meet someone."

Trailing her was an attractive brunette. "This is Margo. She's going to volunteer with us too," said Edie.

Margo smiled. We exchanged pleasantries before she and Edie headed toward the barn.

"That girl is smokin' hot," I whispered to Sonic after they'd walked out of earshot. "Don't get any ideas about her, buddy." I patted his neck. "You're mine."

A couple days later, I had a Facebook friend request from Margo. She was a high school guidance counselor getting her masters in social work. I discovered she hoped to work with the military population when she graduated.

Margo volunteered a few Saturdays over the next months. She managed to find me wherever I was. I figured she was interested in my military background because of her studies. She was friendly and laughed easily. Her brown eyes radiated kindness, and I wondered if she felt sorry for me.

That April, Edie asked me to speak at a fundraising dinner. She wanted me to tell my story and explain to prospective donors how Quantum Leap Farm helped me.

Margo was there at my table, along with a few other farm staff. As people were finishing their entrees, I went to the stage, held the microphone, and told my story.

Everyone applauded. I was feeling pretty good about myself as I went back to my table. Edie took the stage and closed the event with an appeal for donations for the equine therapy program.

As people were standing to leave, Edie rushed toward me. I figured she was going to praise me on my talk.

She squatted in front of my wheelchair, took my hands in hers, and said adamantly, "If you don't ask Margo out by the end of the night, you're not allowed back at the farm."

What? I thought she was kidding and started to laugh, but Edie's steel blue gaze held mine. She lifted her eyebrows and nodded encouragingly, before hurrying off to a prospective donor.

Funny thing, I wasn't nervous while speaking on stage moments ago, but now I was shaking in my boots. Literally.

Margo walked toward me from the other side of the table. She complimented me on my speech and my Tony Lama boots. I put my hands on my knees to make sure they weren't knocking. Beads of perspiration formed on my forehead while we made small talk. I was so anxious that I don't think my words made sense. Margo said good night and began to walk away. I dug down deep for courage.

> *I exhaled a myriad of emotions, but then doubt and fear barged their way into my mind. I tried not to get my hopes up.*

"Hey!" The word came out louder than I intended.

Margo turned.

"We should get something to eat sometime." After I said it, I held my breath.

"Sure," she answered, her dark eyes shining. "I'd like that."

I exhaled a myriad of emotions—relief, excitement— but then my constant companions, doubt and fear, barged their way into my mind. *Would a girl like that really want to go out with me?* I tried not to get my hopes up.

That Saturday afternoon, I picked up Margo for pie and coffee. We talked for hours. She was everything I imagined, more than I ever dared to hope for. Intelligent, witty, beautiful, optimistic, understanding. When I drove her home, I leaned over and kissed her cheek. I couldn't help but feel a smidgen of encouragement.

The next week at the farm, Sonic nickered when I rolled into the barn. After my ride, I brushed him down.

"I wanna marry that girl Margo," I whispered, as I stood near his face and groomed his neck.

Sonic's ears swirled to the side, toward me, as if he were considering the idea. His steady gaze made me think he approved. Simultaneously, a herd of doubts galloped through my mind. *What if Margo realizes my limitations and discounts me like Jess did? Do I really want to risk getting my heart broken again?*

That Sunday, Margo invited me to her church. We met for dinner the following week. I felt myself falling hard. She seemed to like me too. But as strong as my feelings were for her, stronger still was my insecurity. I just couldn't trust. She seemed too good to be true.

One Saturday night, Margo came to my apartment for dinner. She asked about my walker in the corner by the door.

"I don't use it much," I said, stirring the pot of venison taco soup. "But if we ever got married, I'd have to use it. I'd want to be on my feet."

Margo's eyes opened wide.

Dude! I berated myself. *Why did you say that?*

Despite my bold remark, we had a wonderful dinner. After she left, I rolled my wheelchair to the walker, grabbed the handles, and stood.

Whether I got married or not, I knew I still had something I needed to prove. And the person I needed to prove it to most of all was me.

Even though I was disabled and medically retired, I was still a soldier. I might be in a wheelchair, but I was still the same risk-taking, adventure-seeking Mark Lalli I'd always been.

Each time I got on the back of Sonic, I lifted my hands, closed my eyes, and gave my trust to a 1,000-pound horse. Now I needed to do the same with God. I needed to drop the reins of how I thought my life "should have been" and trust Him to lead me through the "more" He had for me.

Happily Ever After

Margo and I continued to see each other regularly that summer. We went to Sunday services at her church and usually had a couple dates during the week. Sometimes we'd take in a movie or go out to eat with friends. Occasionally, I even cooked.

That fall, she went back to South Carolina to finish grad school. I took advantage of her absence and resumed weekly physical therapy with the goal of traveling one hundred feet with my walker. The exercises I did daily were hard and painful, but I knew it would be worth it. I also continued equine therapy with Sonic. I was sore twenty-four hours a day, seven days a week. With Margo gone all week, I was able to keep my goal of walking a secret.

Even with Margo away many weekends, I continued attending her church. One Sunday after services, the minister said they were doing baptisms. Naturally, in the Episcopal Church I'd been baptized as an infant, but I was curious about how these immersion baptisms worked. I watched a few people cross their arms over their chest as the minister leaned them back in the water.

On my way to my car, a strange awareness washed over me. *I need to do this.* I wheeled around and got in line. When my turn came, the minister put an arm around my back and submerged me. When I came up out of the water, everyone cheered. I pumped my fist in the air. It was the new beginning I needed.

A couple months later in December, when Margo was home from college, I cooked for us again. Her favorite Christmas movie was *Rudolph the Red-Nosed Reindeer,* so I put the Blu-ray Disc in after we ate. Snuggling with her on the couch in front of the television screen, I took a deep breath.

"Margo, these months with you have been a dream come true," I said. "I love you. I want to spend the rest of my life with you."

"Shh...." she said, a little annoyed that I'd interrupted the movie. "This is the good part."

I waited until the scene was over and tried again.

"Margo, I want to marry you."

I pulled a ring out of my shirt's chest pocket. A jeweler back home had designed it for me. I took her hand in mine.

Two years after we met, Margo and I married at the farm. Sonic was there too, and I walked down the aisle all by myself with my walker.

"At the beginning of this year I asked God to send me an angel. I believe that's you. Will you marry me?"

"Oh my gosh," she exclaimed. "Yes!"

We hugged.

Through tears Margo added, "I've been praying for someone special too!"

Two years after we met, Margo and I married. Of course, our wedding was held outdoors at the farm. Sonic was there too. I saw tears stream down the cheeks of family and friends as they watched me walk down the center aisle all by myself with my walker. But the thrill of me walking paled in comparison to how I felt standing at the altar and exchanging vows with my radiant bride, Margo. After the minister pronounced us husband and wife, we kissed, then turned to face our friends and family.

In their eyes, I saw that the message God had given me when I visited the other realm had been answered—God had more for me—more than I could ever dream or imagine! (Ephesians 3:20) God had sent me an angel, Margo, to share my life with.

Three years after our wedding, God blessed us with twin girls. My little "lady babies," Cassidy and Phoebe, are now two. I'm enjoying the ride of my life, living in God's promise of hope. I celebrate each Alive Day being all that I can be because of the future God has for me.

My Life since My
Near-Death Experience

Mark Lalli

In addition to keeping his faith and trust in God primary in his life, Mark credits Wounded Warrior Project (WWP) for helping him out of the dark place he was stuck in after the accident.

Q *How has Wounded Warrior Project helped you with your physical and emotional recovery from the accident?*

A WWP started in 2003 as an organization that provides comfort items at the bedsides of injured veterans. WWP has grown to connect warriors, families, and caregivers with healing programs and services. For seventeen years, its focus has been building long-term veteran support structures that empower warriors on their paths to recovery.

Members of WWP have done everything from taking me out to ball games and getting me involved with the community. And my work in the organization has gotten me to the point where I can mentor other warriors, speak to their families, and provide the right resources to get them back in their communities.

Q *What is one of the proudest moments of your life?*

A PJ, my high school best friend, joined the ROTC at the University of Dayton. When a new officer gets commissioned, he picks a noncommissioned officer to be his first salute and be part of a "Silver Dollar" Salute ceremony. This tradition in the army where a newly commissioned officer presents a silver dollar to the first enlisted soldier who salutes them was started by General George Washington in the Revolutionary War. The idea is that every commissioned officer in the army would have a sort of right-hand man.

I was still in rehab at the time, so I flew to Cleveland from Tampa and participated in the Silver Dollar Salute. It was pretty awesome; the silver dollar is on a shelf in my office now. I was also PJ's best man in his wedding.

~

Q *How has your NDE changed you?*

A I live every Alive Day trying to be my best self, serving my community, family, and God. Some days it's really challenging, but just because I can't walk doesn't mean I can't serve or enjoy life.

I believe it was God who led me to Wounded Warrior Project. I am very involved with WWP in helping other vets. I also participate in adaptive sports through that organization. I play sled hockey, wheelchair softball, tennis, and basketball.

Together, God and WWP gave me my life back—a life worth living.

Heavenly Hosts

By Sharon Milliman, as told to Guideposts

Do not conform to the pattern of this world, but be transformed by the renewing of your mind. Then you will be able to test and approve what God's will is—his good, pleasing and perfect will.

Romans 12:2 (NIV)

All my life, I have been drawn toward the light. As a little girl in Ohio, I liked nothing better than to play with the sunbeams that streamed into my room during the day.

Many children are intuitively afraid of the dark. Perhaps, somehow, they know to fear darkness and seek light long before they ever understand what good and evil are. All I know for sure is that when I was only about three years old, the darkness terrified me. When night fell and I was alone in my bedroom, I yearned for the sunbeams to return.

Then, one night, it happened for the first time.

Angels came out of my closet. One by one, they came out and stood around my bed and began singing sweet lullabies. Some held what looked like candles; others carried boxes made of gold. Their beautiful, soft light and sweet songs chased away my fears and lulled me to sleep.

This was only the beginning of the many encounters from beyond that I would have for the rest of my life.

Childhood Friends

I do not know the names of the angels who surrounded my bed at night when I was a child, but another special spirit, whose name I did know, began appearing to me around that same time.

I called him Jonas, and my parents thought of him as my imaginary friend. The truth was, his real name was Michael, and he was my brother who had died in infancy.

Michael was born when I was just one year old. He died at the hospital before ever coming home. A year later, my mother lost another son, Stephen, when he was stillborn.

It was always sad to me that Michael and Stephen had missed out on growing up in our all-American Catholic family. My two sisters and I were blessed with wonderful parents. Dad was a strong yet gentle presence in our home, and Mom was deeply devoted to God and the Virgin Mary. Dad traveled a lot for work, and Mom stayed home and took care of us. Each day after school, I could hardly wait to get home, where Mom would be waiting at the front door to scoop me into her tender embrace.

I missed Dad terribly when he was away. He always seemed to be able to right every wrong, and in my eyes, he knew the correct answer to every question. I felt frightened when Dad wasn't there, but even at a young age, I felt a great sense of responsibility to be strong and to take care of Mom. Even through her cheerful demeanor, I could sense the deep hurt she felt inside from losing Michael and Stephen. I don't believe the pain of a loss like that ever truly goes away. When Michael started to visit me from beyond the grave when I was about four years old, I knew who he was, but I was afraid to tell Mom for fear that it would upset her to think about him.

That's why I began calling Michael by the name of Jonas.

When I told Mom and Dad that I was playing with Jonas, they thought it was cute that I had an imaginary friend. But Jonas was far from imaginary. He was as real and solid as any other person in my life.

Jonas came every day to play with me, and we had so much fun together. He appeared to be about my age, with blonde hair and blue eyes. He loved making a little mischief. One time, when Mom made brownies for the church bake sale, Jonas

> *Jonas was far from imaginary. He was as real and solid as any other person in my life.*

and I snuck a couple for ourselves. When Mom discovered me with chocolate crumbs all over my face, I told her, "Jonas did it." Mom sent both of us to my room, where we played with my stuffed animals until our punishment was over.

I knew that Michael had been sent to me to be my friend. I had always been different than other children and never felt like I fit in anywhere. I don't know why—maybe it was because I had almost died in infancy, like Michael, when my mom had tripped and gone into early labor. All I know is that, even as a child, I felt that I had been born out of my proper time, as though I belonged in another century, perhaps. I never made friends at school. Each school day, I would throw up, terrified to leave my mother's side, afraid that she needed me to take care of her somehow. Because of all this, I think that God, in His kindness, sent Michael to me to be the friend I so desperately needed.

Just before I turned six, our family moved. Sadly, Michael did not go with us. I didn't know it then, but I would see him later, when I was older.

Finding Comfort

A few years after we moved, one of my sisters nearly died from a kidney disease. She got better, but her illness only increased my sense that I had to take care of Mom. She had already been through so much.

I suppose that I worried most about Mom when, the following year, I myself became extremely ill. I came down with a 106-degree fever. Dad was out of town working, so Mom had to take me to the hospital alone. There, the doctors and nurses rushed to put me on an ice mattress to try to bring down the fever. For two weeks, no one knew what was wrong with me, and I was kept in isolation. Even Mom was not allowed to stay with me during that time, so there I was, at the age of eight, alone and afraid in a big, strange hospital.

> *I would awaken to find him sitting in the corner of my room, surrounded by a bright, golden light. I knew he was an angel.*

Each day, a young man came to take me for a chest X-ray. He was always kind and never failed to make me laugh. After the X-rays, he would stay and visit with me for a few minutes. Late at night, I would awaken to find him sitting in the corner of my room, surrounded by a bright, golden light. His presence made me feel safe. He never spoke and would vanish when I looked away. That's how I knew he was an angel.

The doctors determined that I had inhaled a spore that had lodged in my lung. The spore had multiplied, and that was why I'd become so sick.

One day after an X-ray, my angel put me back in my hospital bed, touched my hair, and told me that I would get well. Just a couple of days later, the doctor said I was well enough to go home.

For me, the angel's presence confirmed my innate sense of God all around me my entire life. From the time I'd been playing with sunbeams in my bedroom, I could feel God's presence. I could sense Him in the storm and in the rainbows that would appear in the bluish-purple sky after the rain. I remember wanting to climb those rainbows up to heaven and be with God.

It was no wonder, then, that when I was about ten years old, I made the conscious decision to make Jesus Lord over my life. I would trust Him to see me through this life and into the next. I had no idea, though, that I would be crossing the bridge between those lives so soon.

Going Under

I can't explain why, but when I was thirteen and taking swimming lessons at the local YMCA, I had a terrible sense of foreboding when my instructor told us to dive in at the ten-foot-deep side of the pool. The other kids did as they were told and came out just fine; I was the only holdout. "I'm not ready," I insisted.

"You will dive in or I will throw you in," my instructor threatened.

I walked to the side of the pool and tried to make myself dive in, but I just couldn't do it. All of a sudden, I felt my instructor's big hands on me, shoving me into the water.

Terrified, I fought against the water, sinking farther and farther down, all the while taking more and more water into my lungs. After what seemed like hours of sinking, I reached the bottom of the pool.

All at once, I was no longer scared. I felt no pain or fear, and time seemed to stand still, even though I could hear people screaming. I saw my mother standing on the balcony at the opposite end of the pool, also screaming in terror. I shouldn't have been able to see her from my vantage point, but I could. I could also see the face of a young lifeguard who was at the other end of the pool teaching young children. She yelled at my instructor to dive in and get me, but he was frozen in fear. Meanwhile, the top of the water rippled and moved in slow motion, and I could see the glow of a brilliant light above it.

As the light began to move slowly toward me, it seemed to exude love.

> *The top of the water rippled, and I could see the glow of a brilliant light above it. The light seemed to exude love; I felt warm and safe.*

Bathed in this light, I felt warm and safe. Strangely, the intensity of the light did not burn my eyes. As the light began to move faster and closer to me, I felt a need to surrender to its embrace. Just as the light was about to touch me, I heard the harsh sound of a metal door slamming shut—then a sudden excruciating pain in my chest.

A lifeguard had jumped in and pulled me from the pool. I began coughing, throwing up the water in my lungs. I began shaking with fear and pain. Finally, after several minutes, I was able to breathe normally again. But I knew what I had experienced was anything but normal.

Long after that day, I wondered what that beautiful light had been. I never told anyone, not even my parents, what I had experienced. I knew that the light had changed me forever. It would take me several years, though, before I realized that the light I saw was God, that I had had a near-death experience.

An Unforgettable Encounter

Not only did I keep my experience with the light to myself, but I also kept many other secrets. The following year, I was the victim of a child predator, and I never told anyone. Although that horrible experience shattered my childhood innocence, I was comforted by visions of spirits, the most welcome of whom was my brother Michael, who had finally returned to me after such a long absence.

As glad as I was to see Michael again, I told no one about him either. I was afraid people would think I was crazy, and, frankly, there were times I questioned my own sanity. During my adolescence, my self-worth plummeted. I had always been a quiet child, but now I was becoming more and more withdrawn, isolated, and afraid. At times, I even thought about taking my own life.

On Good Friday of my fifteenth year, our youth choir was scheduled to sing at a church service. As we sat and waited in the church basement, I saw a man with a slim build walk into the room. He was so beautiful that I was speechless. He had long, dark wavy hair that came to his waist, an olive complexion, and dark brown eyes. His short beard was neatly trimmed, and when he smiled, he had a dimple. Even though he was dressed like most of us, wearing jeans, a white button-down shirt, and boots, I sensed that I was in the presence of great holiness.

As the man walked closer to me, I somehow knew he was Jesus. It struck me as odd that He would be dressed as He was instead of wearing a white robe, but I supposed His clothing made Him more approachable. I stared at Him as He walked over to me and asked, "Where do I go to sit?" I couldn't answer because my mouth went dry and my brain couldn't form any words, so He just sat down next to me and smiled.

Two older women who were sitting in front of me heard His question and turned around to tell Him where to sit in the church auditorium. Two younger women saw Him also. But while the first two women were telling Him where to sit, He looked at me the whole time. Then He spoke to me.

"What happened to you did happen," He said in a reassuring voice. "You are not crazy. I love you. I will always love you. I will never leave you. You are not alone. Don't be scared." Then He stood up.

As he stood, He touched the elbow of one of the older women in front of me. She had suffered from severe arthritis in that elbow for years and had been unable to bend her arm. Suddenly, her elbow was healed. She exclaimed, "I can move my arm! It's not hurting anymore!"

> *"I will always love you. I will never leave you. Don't be scared."*

Three of the ladies who saw Him have since passed away, but the remaining witness and I still stay in touch and continue to be astonished by what happened. All five of us knew that man was Jesus. We asked others who were there if they had seen Him too. After all, He was right in front of them. Amazingly, none of the other choir members had seen Him.

Heavenly Visitors

It would be some time before I saw Jesus again, but in the interim, I had angelic visitors who came to my aid when I needed them.

In 1982, when my older daughter was still an infant, a grease fire started in our kitchen. Despite my best efforts, I couldn't put it out, so I grabbed her and ran outside. As I stood watching the smoke billow out the front door, I saw a tall man wearing a black trench coat and jeans walking in our neighborhood. I was certain I'd never seen him before.

The man walked over to me and asked if he could help. I told him the smoke was coming from a fire in my kitchen. The man walked into my apartment and was back out in only a minute. There was no way he could have gotten to the kitchen and back that quickly, let alone put out a fire. And yet, he announced, "The fire is out." He asked if I wanted him to stay and help clean up.

"No, thank you," I said. I turned to look at the house for only a split second, and when I looked back, the man was gone.

Eight years later, I was driving across an icy bridge with my daughter when the car spun out of control and rolled over and over. My seat belt broke during the flips; my face hit the steering wheel, and my head smashed through the windshield. As my daughter screamed and metal crunched, I called out, "Dear God, help us!"

Our car slammed into a hillside by the creek. An old, abandoned farmhouse sat at the top of the hill. Although the house had been condemned years before, there were several people living there. They rushed to us and surrounded the car. A man lifted my daughter out of the back seat. Amazingly, she was unhurt. He wrapped her in a blanket, gave her candy, and tucked her into his warm truck. Another person ran to call my family and an ambulance, even though no one ever asked me for the numbers. A woman with eyes as blue as the sky held my head in her lap and wiped blood from my face. "Am I going to die?" I asked her.

"You will live," she responded.

When my sister and the ambulance arrived, I looked around for the lady with the blue eyes so I could thank her before I was taken to the hospital, but she and all the other people were nowhere to be found. My head and facial injuries also miraculously vanished. I knew then that the people who had come to our aid were not people at all, but angels. To this day, I do not bear a single scar from the accident.

Nearly a decade later, a different group of angels came to my aid in another life-threatening situation. A young man I knew was at my house, and he became extremely angry and threatening. He picked up a thick wooden cane that had belonged to my great-grandmother. Just as he was about to strike me with the cane, three angels, each about eight to ten feet tall, appeared. They wore armor and held shields and swords. I knew my would-be attacker saw them as well because he stopped dead in his tracks and his eyes became as big as saucers. He fled, and when he left, so did the angels. The danger had passed. The young man never bothered me again.

> *I knew that the people who had come to our aid were not people at all, but angels.*

A Second Near-Death Experience

By the time I was forty-three, thirty years had passed since the day I'd nearly drowned in the swimming pool. One near-death experience is uncommon enough, but little did I know that I would have two.

It was evening, midsummer 2005. I was sitting outside on the patio steps, chatting on the phone with a friend who lived in Oregon. My husband had just gotten home from work, and it was just starting to sprinkle. I heard thunder in the distance but it sounded so far off that I remained outside. About five minutes later, I heard a loud crack as a lightning bolt lit up the entire sky, and then suddenly I felt a searing pain in my right arm and throughout my body. I'd been struck by lightning! It knocked me to the ground, leaving charred marks on the concrete steps where I'd been sitting. The lightning passed through me to a transformer near the house, causing a neighborhood blackout.

As I lay on the ground shaking, sweating, and nauseated, I felt excruciating pain in both my arm and my chest. Then I felt a force begin to pull me out of my body. It is difficult to describe, but it was as though I were being peeled like a banana, separated from my body.

I found myself floating inside my house. From my vantage point above, everyday items in my home looked strange, and the scene was bathed in a burnt yellow color. It was then that I realized that the furniture was not my furniture, and the curtains were not my curtains. My husband and children were not there. I could hear a radio program playing what sounded like a broadcast from a bygone era. I stopped floating and walked in what seemed like slow motion. I looked for the source of the sound but could not find it.

As I was standing in the living room, a presence appeared. This presence was bigger than my entire house yet was formless. My fear instantly vanished—I knew this presence was God. He put His arms around my waist and held me tightly, and I was filled with love and peace. On every side of me were clouds—beautiful, fluffy pink and gold clouds—and suddenly we flew through them, not up or down, but sideways. As we flew through this cloud tunnel, I felt a deep sense of peace and complete love. It felt as though God's great love was seeping into every pore of my body. I felt complete and totally accepted by His presence, as though I had become part of Him.

Suddenly, two young men, who looked to be in their twenties or early thirties, appeared on either side of me in the clouds. They were both blonde-haired and blue-eyed, and they both wore cream-colored linen clothing. At first, I thought they were angels, but I soon realized that they were my younger brothers who had died as babies. I could tell by the way they looked when they smiled—just like my father. The three of us felt so happy at this family reunion, and I told them how proud of them our father would be. I found myself zeroing in on the linen fabric they wore, and I thought of how the weaving represented the interconnectedness of all things.

> *Rather than being shocked or disturbed by the news of my death, I instead felt overwhelmed by the beauty I witnessed.*

"You've died," my brothers said in unison. I saw their mouths moving when they said it. It could have been that they were speaking telepathically and just moving their lips for my benefit; I don't know. They didn't have to tell me I was in heaven. I already knew.

I looked down the front of myself to see if I still had a body. I did. I was even wearing the same clothes I'd had on when I'd been hit by lightning. And yet I was not the same person at all. I was me, but an improved version—young and vibrant like I'd been in my late twenties.

Rather than being shocked or disturbed by the news of my death, I instead felt overwhelmed by the beauty I witnessed. I could hardly take in the array of colors as Michael and Stephen walked with me from the clouds to a garden with an old stone wall accented with pink roses. I could hear birds singing and water babbling in a stream. As I walked through the soft grass, touched and smelled the flowers, and gazed in awe at the majestic trees, I felt incredible joy at the wonders around me.

But the garden alone was not the fullness of heaven; there was more. The garden was situated to the left of a huge, glorious city. From where I stood, I could see marble buildings with tall columns, each attended by angels. One large building had a golden dome. I somehow understood that each building had a purpose. Some had glorious pools of healing water for souls that had died a traumatic death. Others were exquisite libraries and schools designed for spiritual growth.

Heaven, it seemed, was an active realm where spiritual work was the lifeblood. People were everywhere in this city, and all of them looked to be in their late twenties or early thirties, all the picture of health and happiness. I saw no crying, no suffering, no disabilities or sickness.

I cannot explain how I was able to see inside these buildings while standing in the garden, but it was as though I was somehow able to enter each building and look around. I could see a full 360 degrees around me without even turning my head. My heightened senses gave me an awareness of everything. It was as though I was seeing with spiritual eyes instead of physical ones.

I toured huge, lavish banquet halls with exquisite tables set with the finest meats, cheeses, breads, and fruits, even though food is not needed to sustain life in heaven. It was there strictly for enjoyment. One banquet hall was extravagantly decorated with mahogany walls, with breathtaking paintings hung in heavy, ornate frames. The marble floor, polished to a glassy shine, had a pink area rug. A huge crystal chandelier hung from the ceiling. In the corner sat a magnificent piano, adorned with a golden candelabra and a crystal vase full of huge roses.

People in the finest clothing and jewels moved about the room, taking long-stemmed crystal glasses of champagne from a butler in a tuxedo, all talking and smiling. Some of them danced to the music from the piano. At the other side of the room was a table covered in white linen, lavishly decorated with gorgeous flowers of every color of the rainbow and huge, golden candelabras.

Back outside the buildings, beyond the city walls I saw fertile rural areas with grasslands, rolling hills, and prairies where animals such as chickens, horses, and cows, as well as cats, dogs, and turtles, were roaming freely. Although I did not see any of the many animals I had loved throughout my own life, I smiled as I realized that those we had cherished on earth were waiting for us in heaven. Several houses, some larger than others, were nestled among the trees on grassy hillsides, with lush flower gardens behind them. Some of the houses seemed to be made of a stone that changed color with the rays of the sun. Other houses seemed to be made of crystal and sat on bluffs overlooking an ocean.

> *I smiled as I realized that the animals we had loved and cherished on earth were waiting for us in heaven.*

I began to understand that in heaven, each person determines what he or she wants, provided that the vision does not violate the loving will of God. No one had to tell me this. A sense of knowing and understanding seemed to have been given to me as though I had been hooked up to an IV bottle of divine knowledge. Here, I knew that I could have what I'd always wanted—a home to call my own, to be with my loved ones forever, and to be with Jesus. And yet, no dwelling place was presented to me in the form of the houses I saw, nor did a space at one of the city's buildings seem to have been prepared for me. I didn't mind, though; I would have been perfectly happy to stay in the garden forever.

Back in the garden, the flowers were amazingly bright, and the air was sweet and clear. I could almost drink in the fragrance of the flowers, combined with the sweet smell of freshly cut grass, the musky scent of trees, and the saltiness of ocean water. All the scents came together, and even the air itself was so clean and pure that it had an aroma all its own, similar to the way the earth smells after a fresh rain.

As we walked farther into the garden, other souls gathered around me, and I could feel their love. Some were people I'd seen in the banquet hall; others were new to me. Everyone seemed to be no older than maybe thirty-five. Their skin was healthy and had a youthful glow. It was strange because somehow I felt that I knew all of these people, but I could not place them. All were wearing clothing from different time periods and in different levels of formality: the men and women from the banquet hall wore beautiful gowns and fancy suits, but others wore contemporary, casual clothing such as blue jeans. I decided that each soul was dressed in clothing appropriate to his or her time on earth, and each person was dressed in the way that felt most comfortable to him or her.

They all had one thing in common—they were smiling and happy. And they were all beautiful. I felt at ease around them, as though I belonged, as though we were old friends.

A Life Review

God's presence moved from beside me to behind me. He stood over me, still formless, but I knew He was there. My brothers stood on either side of me as the other souls gathered around. Before I knew it, it was as though a black and white movie on a reel began to play in front of us. The "film" was the entirety of my life, everything I had ever said and done. The other souls who had gathered around had come to offer support, not to judge. Again, this was knowledge given to me as if from an infusion.

The life review was over so quickly that I was stunned. It felt incomplete somehow. I turned to my brothers and asked, "Is there going to be more?" I used my mouth to speak, even though that may have been unnecessary. It seemed that the communication was more mental than spoken. My brothers looked at each other and smiled mischievously, as if they knew something I didn't. I waited for them to tell me what it was, but they never said a word.

> *A white, glowing light radiated from every direction. I somehow knew this light came directly from the heart of God.*

Then I heard God's voice say, "What you put into the universe will come back to you." His voice was not audible but more placed into my thoughts, as though He was sending me a telepathic message. I looked around at the garden and once again took in all the brilliant colors of the flowers, trees, and grass. I inhaled the sweetly fragrant air. Although it seemed like midday, I noticed that I did not see the sun overhead. Instead, a white, glowing light radiated from every direction. From the deepest part of my soul, I somehow knew that this light came directly from the heart of God.

As I watched the flowing stream, its water glistening like diamonds as it cascaded over rocks, and listened to birds singing in the trees, I also heard beautiful music. When I tried to determine the source, I realized it was coming from everywhere. The trees, the leaves, the grass, the rocks, the water—all their unique vibrations came together to create a magnificent symphony praising God. You would think that all these noises combined together would sound incompatible. But that wasn't the case. Everything was in perfect harmony. In that moment, I felt a peace and joy beyond all comprehension.

A Deeper Understanding

I had no idea how long each step of my heavenly journey took because in heaven, there seemed to be no time. In one sense, everything seemed to happen fast, but in another sense, it was as though time stood still. Without my having to ask any questions at all, I began to understand things. Knowledge was infused in me in one aha moment after another. The most puzzling questions of the universe suddenly made clear and perfect sense. I remember smiling and praising God: "You are awesome!" Again, because I was in the habit of communicating verbally, I spoke these words, but I am not sure it was necessary to actually speak.

God's light moved in front of me. I looked down at my body and saw that I had returned to the same form I had on earth when the lightning struck, but I felt much lighter, as if there were no gravity to weigh me down. And I was illuminated, glowing like everything else in heaven! I began to realize that I was made from God's loving energy and that my physical form was of little consequence. God loved and accepted me.

Next, I saw a man walking toward me. He was so beautiful. Even with all the other souls around, I was completely focused on him, as though no one else were there, not even my brothers or God. In fact, I'm not sure where God was at that point. He could have still been with me, but I did not see Him, only the man. The man had dark, wavy hair cascading down his back. He had an olive complexion and warm, dark brown eyes. Most striking, though, was his smile: it completely melted my heart. I knew deep in my soul that this man was Jesus, the Son of God.

> *I had loved Jesus ever since I was a little girl, and now, here I was, standing with Him as He professed His love for me.*

"I love you," He told me. "I have walked beside you every day of your life. I will never leave your side, not ever. Do not be afraid." All I could do was stare at Him, speechless. I had loved Jesus ever since I was a little girl, and now, here I was, standing with Him as He professed His love for me.

Jesus escorted me to a wooded glen at the edge of the garden. Sunbeams poured through the branches of the tall oak and pine trees. I saw a log lying next to a stream and little flowers dotting lush grass. I listened to the birds singing and the water dancing across the rocks. A soft, silken breeze enveloped me like arms holding and caressing me. The peace that filled my soul assured me that this was no ordinary breeze, but the Holy Spirit.

I looked up. Jesus was gone, but a man was sitting on the log. I sat down beside him. He was about six feet tall with shoulder-length, dark, curly hair and a neatly trimmed beard. His blue eyes sparkled as he smiled happily. He wore a white robe and sandals. I somehow knew that this was God the Father and that He was appearing to me in a form that I could approach without fear. For a long time, we just sat together, laughing and talking like old friends. God spoke to me with words, just like a person. I think He did this because He knew that was what I was used to, and He wanted me to feel comfortable.

At one point He smiled and stood up. Then He motioned for me to follow Him.

We walked to the edge of the glen, and He opened the sky as though it had been held together by a zipper. He showed me the whole universe with no one and almost nothing in it—only a black velvety sky with swirling, rainbow-colored gases, sparkling diamond stars, and spinning planets. I gasped at the immensity and beauty of it.

Suddenly, we were back sitting on the log.

I looked out at a large oak tree in front of me. But instead of seeing the tree in its entirety, I saw individual parts: details of the trunk, the life-giving veins in each tender leaf, the roots beneath the ground. I realized how important each part of the tree was to the entire tree's life, and I likened this to the connectedness of the universe. "You made this tree," I said. "You are in this tree, and when I look at it, I see You."

God smiled. "Yes," He replied.

"You made my parents. You are in them. So when I look at them, I see You."

"Yes," He said.

I thought of my husband. We'd been going through the motions of being a couple. Our marriage had been suffering a severe strain ever since I cracked my head on concrete and began having severe seizures, which had caused my husband to become more of my caregiver than my partner. I was convinced my husband no longer cared for me.

But here, in God's presence, my husband's feelings toward me seemed irrelevant as to how I was to view him. "You made my husband," I said. "You are in him. So when I see him, I see You." I now firmly believed with all my heart that I truly could see everyone, including my husband, through God's eyes.

"Yes," He said.

I realized God wanted me to continue to go deeper, and I did—to the point where I realized that all people, even the ones who had hurt me, were made by God.

> *As I gazed into God's eyes and saw the deep love in their infinite depths, my feelings of inadequacy melted away.*

"And when you look in a mirror, what do you see?" He asked.

I looked down at my hands and thought for a moment. Ordinarily, my response to this question would have been, "I am just me. I am no one special."

But as I gazed into God's eyes and saw the deep love in their infinite depths, my feelings of inadequacy melted away. "You made me, and You are in me," I replied. "So when I look in the mirror, I see You."

God smiled at me. Then He picked up a stick and drew symbols in the dirt. I could not discern the meaning of the symbols, but when He looked at me again, I saw in His eyes the fullness of eternity. I felt an incredible peace and love envelop every fiber of my being.

He stood again to walk, and I followed Him through the forest, where two women in beautiful gowns joined us. I knew instinctively they were angels. They led me to a serene lake at the end of the wooded area. There, they began showing me moving pictures of future events on earth—troubling images that shocked and horrified me. Bombings, shootings, terrorist attacks. Financial institutions crumbling. Natural disasters.

Huge waves of water covering the land. Corrupt governments and global wars. Coups and riots. Burning buildings. A huge silver ribbon of a river splitting the United States apart. It was only because I was standing in God's presence that I could bear to see these images. But I also saw angels actively working among these scenes, pulling people out of the water and reviving them or directing them to safe havens in the mountains.

Returned to Earth

No one in heaven explained to me what I was to do with these visions. Before I could ask, I felt an incredible pain radiate from my right arm into my chest. I realized that my spirit was re-entering my body, whether I wanted it to happen or not.

The next thing I knew, I was lying on the ground in my backyard, right next to the steps I'd been sitting on when the lightning hit me. I could see black char marks on the steps. The phone I'd been holding was burned and black, and it was lying on the opposite side of the patio.

I was shaking, sweating, and nauseated. I was in so much pain I could hardly move. I cried out for help, but no one came. I'm not sure how long I lay outside, but eventually, using every ounce of strength I had, I somehow managed to crawl inside the house. I found my husband and told him I'd been struck by lightning and that I was in pain. I asked him to take me to the hospital, but he refused.

So instead of taking myself to the ER, I stayed home. I was disoriented and confused and continued to have pain in my right arm. The next morning, I called my family doctor and made an appointment. He sent me to a cardiologist who ran some tests that showed minor heart damage as a result of the lightning strike. "You might call it an electrical glitch in your heart," the cardiologist told me. "I've never seen anything like it before. You're lucky to be alive." He ran other tests, including neurological ones, but found nothing else wrong.

The Pink Bubble

After several days, the pain in my arm subsided, and I felt better than I ever had in my entire life. I was full of energy and went many nights without much sleep. But instead of feeling fatigued, I was blissfully happy, vibrant, and alive. I felt as if I could see the life force glowing in every living thing. I'd never felt so connected with all of creation and so in love with God. The best way I can describe it is that it was as if I were floating in a pink bubble that could never burst. I call it my pink bubble because everything I saw seemed to radiate a pinkish glow.

My perception of all living things changed after my near-death experience. It was as if my senses were heightened. I could see a beautiful, colorful glow radiating from every plant, flower, tree, animal, and person. I could hear the hum of electricity in the air. I breathed in clear, clean, fragrant air—the same air I breathed in heaven.

While in the pink bubble, I would spend hours sitting in silence while listening, praying, and remembering my experience in heaven. I replayed the conversations with God and Jesus as part of my daily prayers. I could hear heavenly music and even God whispering in the wind. There were many times when I would shake myself, wondering if all of these things I was seeing and hearing and remembering were real. Then the heavenly music would play again, and I knew it was all true.

The pink bubble transformed the way I related to the world, and I began writing poetry about God's gracious love and abundant generosity. I never wanted to forget what I had felt and heard in heaven. Sometimes my remembrances would cause me to suddenly start dancing as a means of expressing the joy and peace I felt inside.

Before my near-death experience, I would have been far too busy keeping house and mothering my teenage children to take time to sit and be in the moment with God. Although I'd always prayed, I now realized that I'd been speaking *to* God instead of *with* Him; I'd never taken the time to sit quietly and listen to His voice. After my time in heaven, I knew that I needed that daily time with God just like I needed food and air.

> *Although I'd always prayed, I now realized that I'd been speaking to God instead of with Him.*

I tried to bring my husband with me on this new spiritual path. I truly hoped that we could both begin to see each other anew, through God's eyes. When I told him all the things that I'd experienced, he announced that he no longer believed in God at all. "If I can't see it or touch it, it's not real!" he snapped. It seemed that my relationship with God infuriated him. He wanted me to stop talking about heaven. He couldn't understand that after having had a face-to-face conversation with God, in heaven, I couldn't relinquish that connection.

I continued to have visions and communicate with spirits. My husband thought I was crazy, and he even convinced my friends and family, including my parents, that I had lost my mind since being struck by lightning. That was true, of course. But I wasn't different because I was crazy, but rather because I'd been touched by God. I knew I was not hallucinating.

Some of the visions were troubling, and I eventually went to see three different priests, searching for answers about why I was seeing spirits and having visions. All three priests told me the same thing: that I had the "gift of angels." None of them, however, could explain to me what this fully entailed, so in a sense, I was even more confused than before I'd sought their counsel.

Meanwhile, my husband had had enough. He announced that he was taking me to the hospital for treatment. I knew arguing would be pointless, so I went.

At the hospital, I saw a kind, soft-spoken doctor who had a glow about him and a sparkle in his eyes. His aura seemed familiar to me, and I wondered if he might be an angel. "Do you feel you need to be here?" the doctor asked gently. I told him no, and he asked me to explain how all this had come to pass. I told him everything: the lightning strike, the near-death experience, and the visions of spirits since then. When I finished my story, the doctor smiled. "I don't think there's anything wrong with you," he said. He signed my release papers, and my husband grudgingly took me home.

> *At the hospital, I saw a doctor who had a glow about him and a sparkle in his eyes. I wondered if he might be an angel.*

By Christmas of that year, the happiness and joy I'd felt since my near-death experience had been severely taxed by all this conflict. I tried hard to stay in the blissful state of my pink bubble, but I felt betrayed and hurt by my husband's attitude toward me. Before the new year, my pink bubble had seemingly popped. With it gone, all I felt was numbness.

I wanted so badly to go back into the pink bubble, but I didn't know how. I cried often and was extremely unhappy. I felt that my heart had been shattered and that sorrow enveloped my very being. I could not understand why God had sent me back to earth. Why couldn't I have stayed in heaven? I was falling into a dark pit of despair, especially as things got worse with my husband. I had seen heaven, and I knew it was real, so I felt no fear of dying. So why couldn't I just leave? My daughters had moved out and were busy with their own children; no one needed me here.

As another new year began, the perfection I'd experienced in heaven seemed only to underscore the turbulence of my earthly life. My marriage was dissolving right before my eyes, and people seemed to be so mean and selfish, so unlike the pure love I'd experienced in heaven.

I pleaded with God to let me leave this world, yet deep down, I felt He had a special mission for me here. I just didn't know what that mission entailed.

In the Garden

In the midst of these trials, however, God comforted me in many ways. One day, I was sitting outside in the backyard, enjoying the soft spring breeze. I heard a noise and looked up to see Jesus standing by the fence next to the flower garden as the sun shone down on Him. He wore a long, flowing, cream-colored robe and sandals. He smiled at me and stretched out His hand. In it was a stemless pink rose. As He offered me the flower, He spoke to me verbally for a long time. "This life is a journey that all must take," He said. "Please don't question yourself so much. Stand at your gate and take the rose. It's time for you to fly. Today is a new and wondrous beginning.

"I love you and will always love you. You will never walk alone. Hold your head up high and always spread your joy and love. Open your heart and don't be afraid. Just cast all your fears aside and accept your new life."

Then He handed me the pink rose. It was made of silk so that it would never wither. I still have that rose today, tucked away safely. Every time I look at it, I am reminded that I never walk alone.

Angel in the Woods

Even though Jesus had visited with me in my garden, I longed to find a sense of peace and oneness with God every day, and I often sought it outdoors. One day, I walked into the woods and sat down on the forest floor, watching the sun stream down through the leaves of the tall trees. Suddenly, it was as though my pink bubble had returned and God had lifted the veil of the earth to show me heaven once again.

I heard the cry of a hawk and looked up to see him emerge from the woods. That was when I saw an angel.

Everything around me seemed so full and so much more alive. I could hear heavenly music in the air as a sapphire blue river and a nearby crystal-clear waterfall sang a pure, rich melody in harmony with the songs of birds. The hills glowed a vibrant gold, and the trees hung laden with nuts and berries as deer roamed plentifully. Blue swallowtail butterflies flitted all around me to the delicate wildflowers that peeked their heads through the earth. Thick ferns and lush moss cushioned me like a green velvet carpet.

I heard the cry of a red-tailed hawk and looked up to see him emerge from the thick woods. That was when I saw an angel.

The angel moved swiftly toward me and stood before me in a pure, glowing white light. "I have a message of great importance," the angel said. "God has given you the chance to make something special of your life. You are not the victim of fate. Where you are this very moment is exactly where you are meant to be, by God's design." He spoke at length about the choices all people have to make—how we can stop wars and disasters if we believe in miracles and walk God's path. I sat in silence the whole time, never once interrupting. Finally, he told me, "One loving choice can change the course of your life." Then he immediately disappeared.

A Sad Goodbye

As I continued to struggle in my marriage, angels continued to appear. One day, when I was feeling particularly hopeless, several angels appeared to me as I sat out on the back patio. One of them said, "I know your heart hurts, and that is why I've come to tell you something." He told me my marriage was over and that I had to move on—to "stand in peace," as he put it. He predicted that my husband would soon make all the necessary arrangements to end the marriage. He told me that when the papers were filed, I was to "always love God and never stray from the truth." He reminded me that God had told me in heaven that I would never walk alone. Last, he reminded me that I was an heir to the Kingdom of God, and that I had to get myself together so that I could fulfill God's mission for me on earth.

Soon, the angel's message came true. By the time I was forty-seven years old, my divorce was final, and I would have to start my life all over again. I rented a house and tried to make a fresh start, but there were days when I was so depressed, I could not even get out of bed. At times, I would wonder how I would ever be able to reconcile the turbulence of life on this earth with the perfection I had witnessed in heaven. I tried to spend as much time as possible in God's presence.

New Direction

One day a couple of years later, I sat outside on the front porch of my new home to watch the sunrise when I heard God speak to me. "I am your shelter and your strength during the storms of your life. I am the light that guides you. I love you beyond what your eyes have seen and what your ears have heard. When you can't take another step, it is then that I will carry you. When your hope is gone, I will give you a peace beyond understanding and hold you close to my heart. And when you are strong again, I will set you upon your own feet and forever walk beside you, loving you as you walk into eternity."

God spoke to me: "When you can't take another step, it is then that I will carry you. When your hope is gone, I will give you a peace beyond understanding."

After the reminder from God, I knew I needed to step out boldly and trust that He would take care of me. I decided to give up my new home and move into my parents' house. My mother was battling Alzheimer's disease, and I could help with her round-the-clock care. It was a healing time in many ways. My dad, now free of my ex-husband's influence, believed me when I told him about all I had experienced. As my dad and I repaired our relationship and took care of Mom together, I also consulted a priest, hoping to find help processing the anger and pain that lingered from my divorce.

"Do you consider God to be your friend?" the priest asked me.

"Yes," I answered assuredly.

"Then tell Him what you have told me. God has broad shoulders. He is big enough to handle it. If you truly consider God your friend, talk with Him as you would talk with any close friend. Do it and see what happens."

I went home and prayed for two hours straight, crying and pouring out my heart to God. I went to sleep that night feeling relieved of my burden.

The next morning, I saw a new bird's nest in my parents' dogwood tree. A mother bird sat on the eggs in the nest while the father bird sat in the next tree, keeping watch over his family. I interpreted this as a sign from God that I, too, would be safe in my new "nest" and that He would lovingly watch over me.

A New Love

Two years later, when I was in my early fifties, I met someone at church.

When I'd been living in my own home after the divorce, before moving in with my parents, I'd heard a man's audible voice say to me, "Go back to God." I was confused by what this could mean because I'd never been away from God, as far as I knew. But I realized that I hadn't been attending church for some time. For this reason, I interpreted the message to mean, "Go back to church," so when I moved in with my parents, I started going to their congregation with them.

On my first day back at Mass, my parents and I sat in the back. Mom was likely to get distracted or have to go to the bathroom, so we didn't want to disturb anyone. As the service went on, I noticed a golden aura around the man who was signing the service for the deaf. My father could see that something was happening within me. He looked at me and asked, "Are you having a spiritual experience?" It felt so good that Dad now believed that my experiences were real.

"I have no idea," I replied. I hadn't seen auras since my pink bubble had burst. And yet here was this man, standing up at the altar, enveloped in this beautiful light. "Who is that man signing for the deaf?" I asked my dad.

"That's Gary," Dad replied. "Great guy. He's also the church custodian."

After the Mass was over, Dad asked Gary if he'd show us the new additions to the building. I was happy to meet Gary and felt an instant connection to him because of his aura, but I dared not let myself think of him romantically—I never wanted to have my heart hurt again.

I said goodbye to Gary after the tour and tried to put him out of my mind, but soon, we met again at a birthday party for a mutual friend and wound up talking all evening. After that, whenever he saw me at church, he made a point to talk to me. Dad suggested that I invite him over for lunch, and I did. He seemed like such a wonderful person, but I was scared.

I prayed constantly about my developing feelings for Gary, and God kept telling me it was okay to feel the way I did, but still, I resisted. Meanwhile, Gary pursued me, making me feel special by opening doors for me, sending me flowers, and mailing me cards "just because." When Gary kissed me on the cheek one day, I prayed even more fervently. "Lord, I'm too old to feel this kind of infatuation!" I said. "Show me who Gary really is. Show me if he's the person you want for me." I asked God to send me a sign: if he wanted me to be with Gary, I asked him to show me blue birds; if he didn't want me to be with Gary, I asked him to show me red birds.

The next day, I walked outside to find a pile of blue jay feathers piled on the concrete right outside the fence to the backyard, all facing the same way, as if someone had carefully arranged them feather by feather. I laughed. *I suppose it can't get any clearer than this!* I thought. I called Gary and told him what had happened.

"I understand," Gary said. He had been hurt before too. "I waited twenty years for you, Sharon. I always knew that God would find the perfect person for me."

> *I told Gary my entire story, about the times I'd been to heaven. Gary believed every word I told him.*

I told Gary my entire story, about the times I'd been to heaven, the pink bubble, the visits from Jesus, and visions of spirits. I figured if he couldn't handle it, it was better to find out now. Like my parents, Gary believed every word I told him. "I know you're telling the truth," he said. He never doubted me for a second. Soon after, Gary proposed, and I accepted. I couldn't believe how happy I was again on this earth.

Gary and I married in 2013, and when I look at him, I see God, just as God taught me to do when I was in heaven. Because of this, every day is a renewal of our original wedding vows to love each other unconditionally, the way God loves us. But it isn't just Gary that I see through a spiritual lens—it's everyone. Since my near-death experience, I see human life with more loving compassion. To keep myself focused on this eternal viewpoint, I seek God daily.

Messages of Grace

One day after Gary and I were married, I rose early so that I could pray in the quiet stillness of the early morning. I was so happy in my new marriage, yet my mother was still suffering with Alzheimer's, and I worried about her constantly. I had made a promise to God when I was a little girl that I would take care of my parents when they were older, and I intended to keep that promise. But there were days when I felt as if I failed my mother. The burden of caring for Mom could be overwhelming, especially when I had to watch her mind disappear right before my eyes and know that there was nothing I could do to save her.

I heard God speak: "Do not be afraid. I love you and will never leave you. Give Me your burdens. I am strong enough to carry them."

I poured out my heart to God that morning, and during my prayer, I heard God speak these words: "My grace is sufficient. Do not be afraid. I love you and will never leave you. I am in the ever-present moment. No matter what happens in the world with all its chaos, no matter what consequences may befall, I am in you and all around you. My grace and love are constant, never ending. So be still and know that I am God and you are Mine. Give Me your burdens. I am strong enough to carry them." This message gave me the strength to go on without anxiety about my future and to continue to care for my mother's needs.

Angels in Pink

A couple of years later, in April of 2015, my mom had a stroke and had to be hospitalized. Dad and I stayed by her bedside and talked about the best option for her care. Her health had already deteriorated so much, and now the aftereffects of the stroke would only make her even more helpless. We wondered about the possibility of a nursing home, but we had a difficult time getting a sense from the doctors about what Mom's condition might be going forward.

As the hours passed, I kept feeling that someone—or something—was pushing me into the hallway. I also kept hearing the word "hospice" very clearly, as if someone was whispering in my ear. This continued until I finally walked out of Mom's room and into the hallway. There, I met a woman dressed all in pink, a color that seemed to match her vibrant personality. She greeted me with a big smile and sparkling eyes.

This woman told me about hospice, and she told my dad about the program too. When we finished talking, we thanked her for coming. After she left I realized I wanted to speak with her again, so I rushed into the hallway to catch her. There was no trace of her.

I went to the nurse's station and asked about her, but they said no one fitting that description worked at the hospital. They had never even seen her. It was then I realized that she must have been an angel. It all made sense: she had been glowing in pink, which was my favorite color, and there was no way she could have known about our need for hospice. We enlisted the aid of hospice in caring for Mom once she left the hospital.

Mom died later that same month. The night she died, I went outside and looked up at the stars. They looked like hundreds of sparkling diamonds against a black velvet sky. As I stood looking at them, the stars began to grow bigger and brighter, as if someone had turned up a dimmer switch as high as it would go. I smiled and said to myself, *Wow. Someone just turned on all the lights in heaven so Mom can find her way*. I never felt that Mom's death was the result of God not answering my prayers. I had prayed for her healing, of course, but when she died, I realized that God had answered my prayer in the most perfect way: He had taken her home to be with Him. He had truly healed her completely.

A week after Mom died, I went to the hospital to visit a friend's grandmother who was dying. It was difficult to be there so soon after Mom's passing, but I wanted to be supportive. Being back at the hospital was harder than I expected, and I could feel myself crumbling inside. I had to rush out of the hospital room before I broke down.

> *Suddenly, a tall woman appeared. I could see the pinkish glow all around her.*

In the hallway, I had a panic attack. I could not breathe, and it felt as if the walls were moving, the floor was coming up, and the ceiling was coming down. I tried to run, but the hall seemed to grow longer and longer, and I couldn't find my way to the elevator. I began to sob uncontrollably.

Suddenly, a tall woman appeared; she was dressed all in pink. "How can I help you?" she asked. Through my tears, I could see the pinkish glow all around her, and it made me stop crying.

"I can't find my way to the elevator," I said.

"Come with me," she replied.

She helped me into the elevator, where two more women, also dressed in pink, appeared. The first woman told them to help me to my car, then she disappeared. The other two walked me outside and comforted me until I was able to control my emotions enough to drive home. As I got into my car, I turned to wave goodbye, but the two women had vanished. There is no doubt in my mind that these women were angels from God.

Life in the Present

Over the years, trying to integrate my near-death experiences with my everyday life has proven difficult at times. Sometimes it feels as though I have one foot in this world and the other in the eternal world. But the beauty of the things I've experienced has helped me to not fear death. God has shown me over and over how much He loves me, and I know with all my heart that God sent me back from heaven to show that same love toward others. One of the most profound realizations from my near-death experiences is that God is love and everything that comes from God is love. God still speaks to me through the beauty of His creation. In fact, I think He speaks that way to anyone who is willing to listen.

I know that even though years have passed since my near-death experiences, my journey has only just begun. I am still finding new ways to connect with God through love.

My Life since My
Near-Death Experience

Sharon Milliman

My near-death experiences have completely changed me and trans-formed my whole life. After my second NDE, my marriage ended, and I lost many friends who lived very worldly lives. I learned so much while I was in heaven, and now I live every day doing God's will and spreading the message that God is real and heaven is real.

Q *You said you shared your near-death experiences with your family, but have you shared them with anyone else? What kind of reaction did you get?*

A I never spoke to anyone about what happened in the pool when I was thirteen. At the time, I didn't know how to put my experience into words. After the lightning strike, when I had my second NDE, it was a couple of weeks after the incident before I told anyone. I called and spoke with the friend I was on the phone with at the time of the strike. She was a Native American medicine woman. She was the only one I was able to talk to about what I had experienced. She understood everything I shared with her and was the one who told me that I had had a near-death experience. I didn't even know there was a name for it.

My family noticed that I'd completely changed as a person. I tried explaining it to them, but they didn't understand. My then-husband tried to have me committed. It took many years for my family to understand me.

I also lost many friends because of my transformation. I learned to be very careful about whom I shared my story with. Even though I was blissfully happy because of my experiences, I was also very alone and shunned by many because they didn't understand. It took me over eleven years after my second NDE to finally come out with the whole story. That's when I wrote my book, *A Song in the Wind*.

Q *What has been the biggest challenge in your life since your NDEs?*

A During my second NDE, I died and went to heaven. While there, I felt so much love—love like I had never felt before. I was finally complete and felt whole. I felt completely accepted for who I was. I had spent my whole adult life trying to please others only to find out that I could not please anyone, least of all myself.

While in heaven, I felt so light, so bright there. When I came back to my body, I felt so heavy, and the world seemed so dense. The cruelty of the world was a stark reality. I was filled with so much love, and all I wanted was to share it with everyone and anyone who would listen, but no one would at first. People think that this life, this earth, is all there is. But I know there is so much more. This earth, this life, even with all its beauty, is like a dream. What is real is what waits on the other side.

It was so hard returning at first. I experienced so much pain and confusion here, and all I wanted was to be back in heaven. It has taken many years for me to understand that I can have some of heaven right here if I learn how to see its beauty, if I remember to just love.

Q Do you recall aspects of your NDE that at the time didn't make sense but now do?

A Yes. During my second NDE, I was greeted by my two brothers who had died as babies and appeared to me as fully grown men. They were wearing ivory clothing made out of linen. They showed me the herringbone weave pattern. It seemed important to them, but I didn't understand why. It wasn't until a few years ago that I would understand.

One day a few years ago, Gary was watching a TV show about the Shroud of Turin. I just happened to walk in at the moment a close-up of the weave pattern from the Shroud appeared on the TV screen. It was a herringbone weave—the exact picture my two brothers had shown me when I was in heaven. I dropped to the floor, sobbing. I was sure then that my brothers had shown me the weave so that I knew the Shroud was indeed the authentic burial cloth of Jesus.

Q Why do you think God let you witness heaven and continue to speak with Him when you returned to your earthly life?

A I know that God has a purpose for everything He does. During one of my visits with Jesus after my second NDE, He told me, "Everything that has happened in your life has prepared you for this important job I have for you. When you are tired, weary, frightened, or heavy burdened, just give that all to Me and do what you do best. Just love. That's it, just love."

So that's what I do. I just love and let Him do the rest.